Biraima M. Adam

Baggara of Sudan: Culture and Environment

Biraima M Adam

ISBN: 1478242132
ISBN-13: 9781478242130

DEDICATION

To my parents, I owed to them any appreciation in my education successes, may God rest their souls in Heaven.

Biraima (Bir) M. Adam

Biraima M. Adam

CONTENTS

ACKNOWLEDGMENTS

I acknowledge the valuable, insightful comments and critiques of all members of www.sudaneseonline.com Discussion Board, which turn to us, Sudanese people in the diaspora, a nation without borders. I recognize the congeniality of the owner of www.sudaneseonline.com, who hosted me for nearly a decade to write about Baggara culture, issues and prospects.

I would like to acknowledge the importance of the American public library system, which helped me to do bibliography search, and to obtain the most needed references during writing of this book.

Biraima M. Adam

1 PROLOGUE

Late in 1963 or early in 1964, the author was born in Sudan to a nomadic Baggara family, near to Abu Safifa area, northeast of Kadugli city, the provincial capital of South Kordofan State of Sudan. No one knows the exact timing or precise location of the author's birth date, only almighty God knows! Anonymous birth date and location are the norm for Baggara people rather than an exception. Around the year 1963, it could reasonably argued that only a few Baggara could have birth certificates and even fewer could have formal training if any. None had formal training in the author's family or his extended family before him. Education to the Baggara at that time was almost a social stigma and viewed as one of the ways to alienate their kids from Baggara culture and Baggara way of life. The Baggara culture and their way of life were so dominant to the extent that they excluded anything else. Education was not part of Baggara culture. Baggara culture and their way of life are just revolving around cattle growing and rearing, nomadism and living away from cities modalities and urban culture. With such strong grasp of Baggara culture, most of Baggara youth remained ignorant – even at the time of this book writing. However, the author's father, a man of vision, had a different opinion about schooling. He thought, "School teaches literacy, and that is the only way that Baggara can get a glimpse of what the Government intention is against them". He stressed that: "Baggara can protect their wealth against Government high taxation only if they are educating their young to understand Government letters and how to register complaints". Getting a rewarding job in the future was not part of the author's father vision, nor was it a mainstream Baggara culture. Cattle's rearing was a common way to go for Baggara people. With such a simplistic view about education, the author was braved into a totally alien way to his ancestors or even to his immediate siblings. The author's mother and grandmother had different views that their "sweet heart" would not go anywhere. The author's mother had determined to divorce the author's father if he dared to send her son to school. The author's wealthy

5

grandmother had awarded him goats, and cattle to discourage the author father's desire to send him to school.

Through early childhood, the author had enjoyed the company of his mother and grandmother; he had to ride a camel alongside his mother when migrating from one place to another, and he had to sleep with her in the drangal - Baggara's deluxe bed type where all family members sleep. Once his mother separated him, his grandmother took his responsibility; he had to ride on an ox with his grandmother, and he had to sleep in her dome, and he had to eat food she specially prepared for him. When the author was about six years old, he moved to sleep alongside his fellow boys under trees on open space within the cow's quarters. Throughout the night, they enjoyed the immunity from flies and mosquitoes by cows, and when cows would leave the quarters even in mid moonless night, they had to take their sticks to follow the cows to bring them back to the family quarter. The author had to learn early in his life to walk for hours in dark nights only by himself looking for some stray cow or lost calf. He learnt how to ride on a bull, a camel, to subdue an ox or a donkey, and he used to eating trees' barks, leaves and rhizomes during the late afternoon when rearing cattle or to medicate himself from Malaria disease by eating some trees leaf and barks and drinking puree of *Tamarindus indica* (Sudanese vernacular name: *aradeib*). The author's grandfather was local herbs and ethnobotanical practitioner. He used to cure the author and his peers from multitudes of aliments. The grandfather treated them from Measles with drinking donkey's milk. He used certain tree barks, specifically *Xeromphis nilotica* (Sudanese vernacular name: *shagarat el murfaein.* translated as: *wolf tree*) mixed with sour milk to cure them of rabies. For other aliments: he used to shower them with cattle's or camel's urine or to boil trees leaves such as *Combretum spp.* (Locally called: *habil*) to treat hepatitis.

One of the most exceptional qualities of Baggara people is to learn how to feed themselves in the wilderness. Hunting wild animals and games is one way to feed them. Other ways include to lure to catch large birds such as guinea fowls, to do spear fishing, to practice exchange trades: to barter milk for food crops or to start fire using *Corchorus olitorius* (Sudanese vernacular name: *malokhia*) or *Corchorus capsularis* (Sudanese vernacular name: *karkang*) to open up spaces and to scare out wild animals for hunting. Early in Baggara boys life one has to learn to survive in any circumstances: by digging roots and rhizomes for food or uproot some underground stems to drink their juice as water to quench thirsty. On the other hand, Baggara boys learn how not to be an opportunist – who take every possible chance to get a bite from someone else dish or scout around a camp to catch a meal – very abhorring characters. The boys learn what it means to be brave and courageously to fight back in order to survive.

Wilderness of Baggara country is full of excitements and sometime unexpected events – such as a sudden encounter of stray beast or run into someone barbeque a hunted deer is possible. Although seems to be rough and hard, Baggara transhumance life is exceptionally fulfilling to a nomadic Baggara man: moving freely from one place to another without restriction, hunting in the wild, chasing and flattering with Baggara women, galloping horses, wrestling, dancing during lunar days, and many more are the essence of a relaxing Baggara life.

Once the author had grown up to reach school age, he had to leave his best Baggara life in exchange for school and village life. The author's mother fought her battle courageously with the author's father to spare him from going to school, but the author's father had used all his connections, relationship, and the author's mother' relatives relationships to make his case. The author's mother had to go everywhere to her father, tribal leaders, religious sheikh with no help to avert her son from going to school. For the author's mother, the school was so monstrous that her life doomed and that was how Baggara viewed schooling. The author was snatched away by force from his mother warms during the best time of the year for Baggara nomads - the herding season, to a village far in South Kordofan State, where people are in their worst season - the growing season. There in the village, the author saw as if the world came to an end – the place swallowed in a jungle of dense and tall savannah grasses and vegetation; human and animals wastes were everywhere; it was muddy, filthy and unbearably mosquitoes' infested place. The author's intention was to escape from the village, but willingly he had resisted his desire, later on taking honor of his bravery and courage to withstand all adverse conditions at such young age of around seven years. The author had to pass three months before his mother and grandmother to come a long with Baggara nomads to the village and settled next to the school. The author relieved from daunting life and nightmares. Again, before school closing, Baggara nomads migrated northward due to rains, mud and harmful flies to their animals – at that time the author became mindful of obstacles and challenges ahead and started to take control of his own life and destiny at such a young age. The author's father was his hero in every sense; he never stopped encouraging him, pushing him to reach his next education goal or to ease his situation by bringing in needed resources. The author proved he was a successful student progressively

7

beating up his peers in the class to the point that he became the best student by the sixth grade. At that early age, the author knew how to be successful in his education. By the year 1984, the author was a freshman in one of the prestigious and best university in Sudan – the honorable Khartoum University. A long the way the author had kept his passion for Baggara life - passing every school term in the nomadic camp away from cities. In 1989, the author was the best student graduating among his peers, and in less than a year, the Mediterranean Agronomic Institute in Greece awarded him a free grant to pursue a master degree in Renewable Natural Resources. Once the author completed his master degree, he went back again to lead a nomadic Baggara life for a brief period before the University of Salonika in northern Greece called him back to pursue a PhD in the Department of Genetics and Natural Environment.

In June 15, 1997, a new history made, the author immigrated to the United States of America. He was and has been ever since thrilled by the richness and diversity of American life and culture. In November 1999, the author's wife had joined him in the US and soon they formed a family with adoring kids and the author had changed his profession to Software engineering earning a master degree in computer science, in 2003, from the Marymount University in Arlington, Virginia. In July 17, 2012, the author was back to Sudan to visit his Baggara relatives and kinships. He astounded by the profound difference between his previous Baggara life and his current, new found American life. However, Baggara life remains an alternative easy way of life to heavy industrialization and materialist society. The Baggara life is simple with an extremely slow pace of life in opposition to the fast pace of life in the West. Yet the author found almost a close sense of his own Baggara life and culture right here on the West; the Cowboys culture is a Baggara culture (well let us say similar to Baggara culture). Cowboys hats, the horses, the cows, the dangling ropes, the rodeo (bull riding) are all similar to the Baggara life.

In this book, Baggara Culture and Environment, most of the subjects, and materials crosschecked and weighted against the author own memory dump. This is a genuine narrative of Baggara culture and their way of life.

Bir Adam – Reston, Virginia USA 09/22/2012

2 BAGGARA BRIEF ORAL HISTORY

Baggara are legendary nomadic people of sub-Saharan Africa. Proud of whom they are, Baggara people of Sudan are unique from the general masses of Africans in many respects: ethnically, culturally and historically.

Baggara are ethnically and culturally Arabs; they are Muslims, rigorous observers of the five pillars of Islam, and fluent speakers of Arabic language with their own slanted accent called Baggara's Arabic in Sudan, and Shuwa's Arabic in Chad. They are mostly followers of some sophism sect, such as Ansar sect in Sudan, a sophism sect that led Sudan to freedom during Mahdism's Revolution against British rule in Sudan in the nineteenth century. Yet in contrast to the proper Arabs and similarity to Africans, Baggara are lithe to igneous dark in their complexions and they are cattle herders rather than camel growers.

In 1995, Baggara population estimated about 5 million in Africa (Haskins et al., 1998). Baggara claims savannah region of sub-Saharan Africa as their homeland. They have come a long way in their relation with the nature of sub-Saharan Africa, where they live today. Their genetic ingredients and perhaps their ethnic identity far rooted in one of the most arid part of earth – the Arabian Peninsula. They believe that their ancestors migrated from Arabia to Africa during early days of Islamic missionaries - as part of Arabs exodus to North Africa - perhaps as early as the 12th century.

Most historians believe that Baggara belong to the *Guhayna* group; a clan of Bedouin Arabs who migrated from present day Hijaz region in Saudi Arabia. Baggara traditional oral historians say they originally came from the Arabian Peninsula to Egypt, and then followed two routes to their present areas:

The first group moved southward along the River Nile, as part of the victorious Arabs Islamic missionary led by Abdullah ibn Abi Sarh – a companion of Prophet Mohammed (*peace be upon him*). The mission courageously fought with the Nubian Kingdoms over many years; eventually the mission reached a deal with the Nubians, which culminated in writing the historical treaty of Bactum, which allowed the Arabs and Muslims to bypass Nubian lands, and to settle in its southern fringes, which represent present *Khartoum* and *Jezira* region in the middle of Sudan. As grazing lands became more congested and sometimes scarce for their animals, Baggara gradually moved westward to their present habitats between the White Nile and Lake Chad.

The second group of Arabs' Islamic missionaries moved from Egypt along the North Africa's Mediterranean coast. Part of that missionary stayed in present Tunisia, Libya, Morocco and Algeria. They built prominent Islamic Minarets and mosques – such as building of the sacred *Kirawan* city in Tunisia with its 150 mosques, among them, the *The Great Mosque*, which is truly much revered among the Muslims world as *Al Aqsa Mosque* in Quds city of Palestine or *Al-Azhar Mosque* in Cairo city of Egypt. From Tunisia, part of the Arabs, who later became the ancestors of Baggara, split off and moved across Sub-Saharan desert to settle in present day Lake Chad, Cameron, Central Africa Republic and Nigeria. Afterward, part of this group moved eastward from Lake Chad to settle in Sudan. Mac Michael (1922) and Cunnison (1966) are strong supporters of this view. The rest of the missionary, which was advancing along the North Africa's Mediterranean cost, crossed the Mediterranean sea to present day Spain and the Baggara ancestors presumably became part of the Islamic Umayyad Dynasty in Spain. However, after the downfall of Andalucía, part of them re-emigrated to North Africa; they lived in Mauritania, Niger, Nigeria, Chad and probably Sudan (Adil A. Mahmoud, 2006).

Along their migration routes, Baggara ancestors integrated well with local dynasties or indigenous people - whether in North Africa or sub-Saharan regions. The integration of Baggara into local societies led to rebirth of new Islamic sultanates and kingdoms. The integration further led to transformation of nations and communities through injecting Islamic religion, beliefs and culture. The Arabic language, Arab's culture, and a new way of life became dominant features in the local societies. As Baggara are historically well known as superb horse riders and resolute warriors, they became part of the nations' cavalries and armies wherever they settled. El Tunisi in his book: "My Journey to Wadai" wrote about the Arabs that they were strong arm for the sultan of Wadai, and they were powerful horsemen to the point that they kept most of the booty they would collect during war times.

In Sudan, Khalifa Abdullahi El Ta'aishi was the second in command during the renowned Islamic Mahdism's Revolution in the nineteenth century, which defeated the British in Sudan; and eventually he became the new leader of whole united Sudan after the death of Imam Mohamed Ahmed Al Mahdi - founder of the Mahdism's Revolution.

Along their historical journey routes to their present zones of savannah of Sub-Saharan Africa, Baggara have run through metamorphic changes: they gradually gave up their way of life from camel rearing to cattle growing due to change in environmental and ecological conditions (Cunnison 1966). However, Adil A. Mahmoud (2006) disagreed with this premise, saying it is hard to believe that people change their lifestyle out of nothing. Mahmoud believe that, tribal wars, between Baggara and Khuzam Arabs, which broke over a female camel dispute, led to the defeat of Khuzam Arabs. However, Baggara retreated to jungles, which are not suitable for camels growing, to protect themselves from further retaliations. The female camel (called Fanni camel – *Nagat Fanni*) story has a strong presence in the Baggara mythology and oral history. Whatever the reason was, Baggara took up cattle rearing for their suitability to the environment. Once took up cattle rearing, Baggara found that they have been moving in a seasonal journey, between low and high savannah regions, where there are plenty of water and fodder for their cattle. Camel growers, Baggara's kin, remained in semiarid zones of Sub-Saharan Africa, and they named Abbala – meaning camel herders to distinguish them from Baggara cattle herders. Nonetheless, the terms Baggara and Abbala did not come into existence until the British rule coined the terms in the early nineteenth century to distinguish the two forms of animal husbandry. The term Baggara, therefore, means 'Cattle Herders'; it is a collective name applied to certain Sudanese cattle herding tribes, which have Arabic roots and common ancestral lineage and which live – in general - between the White Nile and Lake Chad. The name Shuwa in Chad coined by the Kanuri people along the Shari River in West Africa, and it means the "Beautiful ones". As such, the name Baggara in Sudan, and the name Shuwa in Chad are among the new metamorphosis that these Arabic tribes have gone through during their settlement in their present zones – the names were unknown before their settlement to Sub-Saharan Africa. Baggara also gave up some of the their lofty Arabian or Iberian princes' dresses to colorful and more casual African styles; they mixed their pure Arabic language with local dialects to the point lead to the emergence of the Baggara Arabic and Shuwa Arabic dialects. Although the premise of common Baggara ancestry has strong advocates, but, recent works by many authors among them Dirar (2001) and Adil A. Mahmoud (2006) have drawn conceivably convincing conclusions that Baggara ancestors came from scores of Arab tribes: *Guhayna. Lukhum. Juzam, Qays Aylan, Tayie* and *Beni Hilal* as ancestors of present Baggara as opposite to the popular views of a common *Guhayna* ancestry.

However, contemporary Baggara strongly inclined to believe that they have common ancestors and still clichéd to their Arabic and Sunni Muslims roots, and they have a lot in common with both Arabs and black Africans, yet they have unique ethnic, cultural and historical differences that warrant their uniqueness.

Geographically, Baggara settle or roam the plains between the White Nile and Lake Chad – the area well known as Baggara country or Baggara belt (Cunnison 1966, Mac Michael 1922). They are distributed across different countries: Sudan, Chad, Nigeria, Cameron, and Central Africa Republic where they have created localized versions of theirs culture, costumes, dance and others. Haskins et. al.. (1995) cited that, Baggara location is in Sudan and Chad between the Nile River and Lake Chad, and their Language is Arabic. Although distributed among different countries, Baggara remain inhibiting similar ecological and climatic zones of savannah region of Africa (Cunnison, 1966); their span extends from scrubby, semiarid, sub-Saharan zones to a rich and high vegetation savannah and further reach to swampy marches such as in the White Nile swamps and the Cameron River basins.

Baggara today live much as their ancestors did, remaining a nomadic people who are continually searching for new grazing land; family and personal lives governed by the Islamic faith and local customs (Haskins et al., 1995).

Notwithstanding Africa weather calamities, Baggara people endure well in sub-Saharan savannah region of Africa - their new found home - to a point that they are remarkably much appear indigenized to the region. Even at the climax of hot or rainy season, they engage in social life, dancing, celebration, migration and go about their normal life affairs without any restraints to the weather conditions. Howeer, sometimes, Baggara retreat to shade or restrict their activities when it is necessary. As goods made for certain purposes, and usually packaged with labels such as "made for", it seems anecdotal that Baggara people are God's creation for Africa tumultuous weather. They are resilient to any weather conditions. They live in their shanty domes only temporarily. On the next day, or so, they tear them off, saddle their belongings on their oxen or camels, hush their animals and move onto the next place where there are plenty of water and pasture. The Baggara are a nation in a continuous movement; they move in the summer heat; they move during winter cold; they move on the darkest nights; they move on the hottest days; they move even when it is raining. They will not stay in one place only if water and grazing are abundant enough to support their herds and there are no harmful flies, mud, or eminent danger of any form to themselves or their animals. If there are harmful flies such as tsetse flies, which outbreak in record numbers in high savannah during rainy seasons, Baggara immediately move out of the area despite there are plenty of water and lush vegetation. Similarly, Baggara move out of grazing area if there is mud, which impede their animal's movement. Moving out of high savannah into low savannah and semi-desert region would last just as long as there are grazing for their animals. Ultimately, they move back to high savannah after rainy season stops in their northern ranges. Baggara have been proudly moving in Round-Robin seasonal migrations, between their summer places and fall grazing areas, for centuries, to the point that such migration become part of their history and culture. They write poems and sing songs praising their way of life.

Baggara people are highly praising and valuing courage, bravery, hospitality, and benevolence. Meanwhile, they are highly disgracing and touting cowardliness, cheapness and mischievous ones. Through history, Baggara proved to be distinguished cow's herders, tenacious fighters and resolute warriors, and superior horse cavalries (locally called *fursan*). Baggara are brave hunters of large games and beast, and expert collectors of wild fruits, honey and gums. In good days, they enjoy festivities, hospitalities and gregarious life. In the worst times, they gear up their adaptive capabilities of survival – they can eat tree leaves, parks, rhizomes, wild fruits and berries, wild rice, and whatever that helps them to overcome the impasse – such as prolonged summer, drought period or hunger.

Nomadism being the mode of their life, Baggara nomads developed distinctive adaptations to their transhumance life. One of their best-known adaptions is their keen knowledge of ecosystems in which they live – they can easily spot underground water where they can dig water wells. Baggara know when they have to move from one place to another; they know what environmental or ecological predicates or triggers that they have to use to know if it is the right time to move. Added to these are their natural intelligence, cunning attitudes, inquisitive manner and unmatched curiosity to be well aware of their surroundings. During British raiding in the 19th century, Baggara would pretend utterly subdued to their captive's orders during daytime. When the night fell, they would dance, chat and appeare just normal while behind the scene cowboys would sneak away cattle herds and women would pack their belongings secretly and eventually Baggara would dissipate away from their captors. In other times, they would fight courageously in large tribal formation or sometimes would form small guerrilla warfare to attack garrisons and forts: they could attack, burn and snatch things away in a quick engagement. Baggara oral historians told that Baggara could have rushed into the woods away from the eminent danger leaving everything behind except cattle, which they dearly love. In many cases, danger could be, in the past times, an attack by British battalions, a pass by Turks troops through their areas or more recently crossing by rebels in large groups. In such cases, Baggara would stay away from their quarters until the danger would be over, or they would abandon them altogether. Other times, Baggara might throw their belongings, or bury them in the ground and rush away from the eminent danger. Baggara grandmothers warn their grandsons not to sleep early had been an attack not to be left sleeping during escape time. Baggara could also change their migration routes if there is a disease ahead or if there is a war.

In recent years, Baggara history is in play again and to it is fullest extend during the war between Northern and Southern Sudan. Sometimes, they fought alongside the national army, in other occasions could establish individual treaties with the rebels; sometimes they avoid war areas or they might untimely move out of the war zone. It seems Baggara life is well adapted to survival in any given situation.

Baggara cherish women, love cattle rearing and tea drinking. It is noteworthy that most of the Baggara cultural elements can easily be identified as revolving around cows, women and surprisingly tea! It is such a crucial fact that acquiring knowledge of what these three elements meant to Baggara could give an appreciable insight of their mentality, morality and social life. Baggara history has shown exceptional Baggara passion for acquiring, owning and rearing cattle; in the past, Baggara can raid other tribes or even raid each other tribes or clans to acquire their cattle in broad daylight by brute force. Once upon time such raiders would be praised for their bravery. Cows - represent their sole wealth; they acquire large herds, not for economic reasons, but just for prestige. Women crush on large herds owners. Tea is their sole and best drink. Baggara drink tea countless times during a day whenever they find it. It is an ultimate hospitality if tea offered by a Baggara man or if one could offer tea to a Baggara person. Whole sets of traditions for *Baramka's* social groups and their anti-groups called *Kamakla* flourish and built around tea traditions. Women, on the other hand, are among the most cherished segment of the society in the Baggara culture, whether in their capacity as aphrodisiac human being (Baggara men loves women), as cheer leaders in festivals as tooters for wars or as praise singers (*hakamat*).

Being nomads, Baggara, always, stay in wilders or small villages away from city modalities and cultural centers. In such a way, they have preserved most of their original Arabic lifestyle, religion and language. However, they remained mostly illiterate; in the past, Baggara know next to nil about education, health clinics, life planning, birth control, and other modern means of living. Women are circumcised; teen marriage is common, and family arranged marriage and fighting to death over women affairs are just few examples to highlight.

3 BAGGARA TRIBES, LINEAGE AND SOCIAL GEOGRAPHY

Numbering over one million in Sudan, Baggara are the largest people group in Western Sudan (Cunnison, 1966). Baggara are primarily nomadic cattle herders; they seasonaly move, and their movements are dependent upon the seasons of the year. According to Cunnison (1966), the Arab nomads of the Sudan and Chad Republics are of two kinds: camel men (called *Abbala*) and cattlemen (called *Baggara*). The Baggara Arabs of Sudan are the subject of this book, however, with occasional references to their kin *Abbala*.

The Term Baggara simply means cattlemen but the Sudanese apply the word particularly to the nomadic cattlemen, who span the belt of savannah between Lake Chad and the White Nile. This belt is the homeland for the Baggara people for centuries. Cunnison referenced above said, "History and environment together shed light on their distribution". In Sudan, while the Abbala lives on the semi-desert part of the region, such as northern Kordofan and Darfur, on the other hand, the Baggara live on their southern fringes, occupying the area roughly between 10 - 13 degrees north and extending well into flood basins of the White Nile to the south.

Baggara people of Sudan are tribal societies. They are identified along tribal lineage as tribes, subtribes (called *qaba'il*), and sub subtribes called (pl: *khoshoum biout; sing: khashum bayt*). There are about eight key Baggara tribes in Sudan: Hawazma, Missiriyya Humr (literally means red Missiriyya), Missiriyya Zurug (literally means dark Missiriyya), Rizeigat, Ta'aisha, Habbaniya, Beni Halba, Awlad Himayd, and Beni Selam. In addition, there are scores of smaller Baggara tribes. Baggara identify themselve as having a common ancestor whose name is Al Juneid. The grandfather, Al Juneid, gave birth to three sons; these were Attia, Heymat and Rashid (al walad). Attia descendants include Hawazma, Missirriya and Rizeigat – who collectively called Attawa, or Awlad Atia. Heymat: descendants include Ta'aisha, Beni Helba, Habbaniya, Awlad Himayd and Beni Selam – who collectively called Awlad Heymat. Rashid descendants include all camel growers of north Darfur and north Kordofan, such as Ziyadia, Hamar, and Kabbabish. The descendants of the two sons: Attia and Heymat are the ones called Baggara today – who has collectively known as sons of Attia and sons of Heymat. Adil A. Mahmoud (2006) gave the following Baggara geneology chart

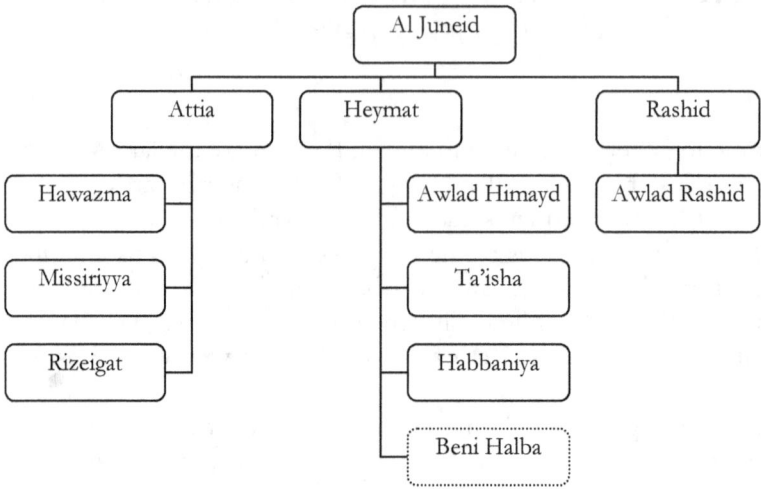

Figure 1: Baggara Genealogy as shown by Adil A. Mahmoud (2006); the author added Beni Halba to the chart.

Baggara have strong social organizations. Cunnison described the Baggara social organization for Missiriyya Humr tribes as follows: "Humr social organization is a segmentary in nature. They are divided into two sections, the 'Felaita' and the 'Ajaira', which are in turn divided into omodiyas, which divided into main sections, minor sections and so on. The dogmatic (generally accepted) model for this structure is an agnatic lineage system, so the members of these groups are in theory all descendent from the one paternal ancestor. Individual camps (*surras*) are themselves lineages and tents within the *surra* organised on the basis of individual families". Cunnison (1966), further shed light on the inner intricacies of Baggara social systems that, "The reality is somewhat different to the theory. In practice, sections have moved around and joined other sections, and these stranger sections considered full members of the higher section they join (though the difference between native and stranger sections may be a line of separation in the event of later disputes within the group). Also, while a group ideally acts as a unit in relations with other groups of the same level, due to internal dissent a subsection of the larger group may ally itself with others".

Omodiyas as described above could be represented pictorially as in the following chart

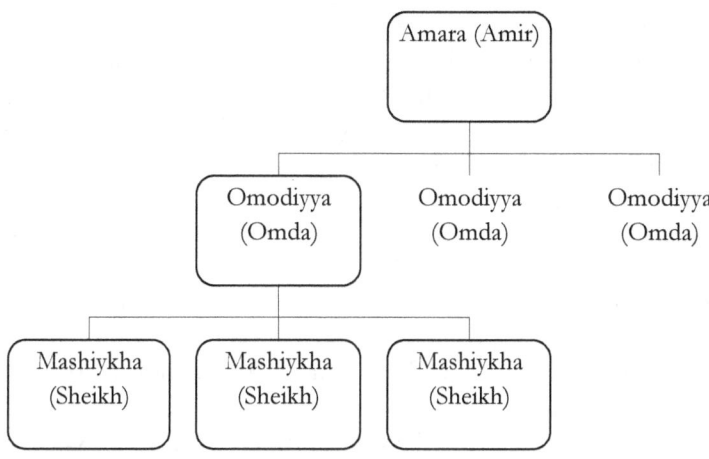

Figure 2: Baggara System organizational chart.

The head of the Baggara social system is *amir* who is the head of his tribe or section. In most cases, each Baggara tribe has one *amara*, which is the legal designation at the level of *amir*. Previous name of *amir* was *nazir*, still today well recognized as a title by all Baggara tribes; similarily, the previous name of *amara* was *nazra*. *Nazir* presides over the tribe. Sometimes there might be more than one *amir* per tribe, for example, Missiriyya Humr tribe of Baggara has two *amirs* – one for the branch of Ajaira and other for the branch of Felaita; hence there are two *amaras*. *Amir* serves as supervisory body of his subordinates, who are called *omad* (sing. *omda*). Each *omda* presides over his *omodiyya*, which is the official title of this post in the Baggara social system. The *omad* resolve most of the cases of disputes within and between different sections, tribes or intratribal issues, but if the case is complex it might require the *amir* attention or to be passed to the official country legal system. *Sheikh* is a ruler over his immediate relatives called *surra*. Elements from different *surras* may join one sheikh, making a large mashiykha, which is the official designation of this post in the Baggara social system at level of sheikh. *Sheikhs* are burdened by tax collection, bringing members issues to the attention of the *omda* and they mediate on issues or crimes that do not require court. The anology could be like state governor (*amir*), the district representive (*omda*) and city mayor (*sheikh*). There is clear distribution of power and responsibilities.

Baggara people of all tribes and agnatic lineages have close physical characteristics, costumes, dance, same Islamic religion, food, and in general, a common culture and life style. They are Sunni Muslims and rigorous observer of Ramadan – fasting.

Based on their way of life, Baggara classified as city or village dwellers, or nomads. Nomadic Baggara main occupations include rearing cattle, in addition to, growing considerable amount of sheep, goats, and camels. They raise horses as means for fighting, trophies, or just for prestige riding.

Geographically, Baggara occupies wide geographic areas between latitudes 10° - 13° N, in case of Baggara of south Darfur they occupy areas between latitudes 7 - 13° N. They have considerable presence in different countries including Sudan, Chad, Nigeria, Cameron, and Central Africa Republic (Adil A. Mahmoud, 2006, Cunnison 1966, Mac Michael 1967).

For such a vast expanse of their distribution, Baggara have resided under different geographic territories, boundaries, jurisdictions, governments, municipalities, and local administrations. They intermingle with a large array of ethnically diverse groupings of people who speak different languages, dress in different styles and eat different ethnic food. Such people include Shilluk people of White Nile, Nuba people of the Nuba Mountains, Dinka people of Abyei area of Southern Kordofan, Fur people of Mara Mountain in Darfur, Kanuri on the Shari River, and others. The vast political, geographic, ethnic and cultural variations along Baggara zones led to considerable variations in Baggara culture and their way of life. For instance, Hawazma, Awlad Himayd and Missiriyya Zurug have adopted the Nuba people wrestling style, while other Baggara tribes have not. However, due to strong grasp of Baggara culture, which mostly draws strength from Islamic Faith and the widely distributed Arabic Language. In essence, Baggara culture becomes one of the dominant cultures in the regions of sub-saharan Africa; sometimes, it becomes norms for the majority of ethnic groupings. Baggara Arabic dialect becomes, in many cases, lingua franca for many societies, such as Shuwa Arabic dialect is the lingua franca for many of Chadian people.

Within the vast span of their geographical territories, Baggara migrate seasonally, north to south, or vice versa, between pasturelands in their northern ranges during the rainy season and riverbeds areas in their southern ranges during the dry seasons. The northern ranges are rainy season graizing zones, while, southern ranges are dry season grazing lands. Cunnison (1966) stated that, whenever Baggara move north to south, or laterally, east to west, they still, inhabit similar ecological and climatic zones. Northern ranges of Baggara zones are semiarid, low savannah regions, where vegetation type mostly dominated by scrubby tree formations, which is characteristic of savannah steppes or Sahel, with much of the areas being sand dunes or undulating plateaus. Rainfall is low in northern ranges between 300 – 450 mm (11.8 – 17.7 inch) annually and temperature can reach as high as 40 – 45 °C (104 – 113 °F). Southern ranges of Baggara zones reach high rainfall savannah regions where rainfall typically ranges between 600 – 800 mm (23.6 – 31.5 inch), with typically high forest with closed canopies, and sometimes, swampy riverine vegetation.

Usually, Baggara across their ranges have two seasonal movements: from south to north during the rainy season (called *tadali* journey), where they migrate approximately more than 300 – 500 km (~ 200 - 300 miles) twice a year (Flint and De Waal, 2008). During such a long journey, they quarter their camps in more than 30 different places until they reach their final destination. Sometimes, Baggara migrate over one month journey before they reach their destination. To add those days where they take rest during their migration, Baggara can take up to two months to complete their journey. At the beginning of a dry season, Baggara reverse course; they move back to their summer grazing ranges (this is called *mou'wota* journey), passing through different routes but with approximately similar places and time span.

Through seasonal transhumance migration, Baggara pass over diverse trains, ethnic groups, landscapes, vegetation types, and climatic zones. They interact with different ethnic groups: barter milk with crops, sell to them live animals and buy grains from them. They engage in dance, festivities, and other events. Since Baggara move between fairly civilized, developed areas, such Northern Kordofan, and poor, underdeveloped areas, such as South Kordofan, Baggara become strong force of cultural modernization to the underdeveloped parts of their grazing zones. Baggara costumes are widely adopted by many local groupings in the   poorer and underdeveloped areas.

BAGGARA TRIBES

Geographically, all Baggara of Sudan are part of Northern Sudan. They share the area between the White Nile and Southern Darfur with many other groups in the regions. Following is a brief description of each of their major tribes georghically arranged from the most eastern Beni Selam tribe to the most western Ta'aisha tribe. Notice is made of their social georgphy and companion non-Baggra tribes.

BENI SELAM:

(Synonyms: Beni Selim, Benu Selaym, Banu Sulaym) are the most eastern tribe of Baggara fraternity of Sudan. They either live in villages or migrate seasonally between the White Nile State of Northern Sudan and the Upper Nile State of Southern Sudan. They are located south of Kowsti city, of Northern Sudan. El-Rudays area is their northern ranges. They move from El-Rudays southward through areas such as El-Jory, El-Naem, El-Rashidi, Um Jallala, and El-Kuwaik to the Tonj area (riverbeds and swamps) in the southern part of Upper Nile State of Southern Sudan, where they interact with Shilluk tribes in the South and share with them the land for many generations since Baggara settled in Sudan. The Shilluk (*Chollo*) is a large Nilotic tribe of Southern Sudan, living on both banks of the White Nile in the vicinity of the city of Malakal (from *Wikipedia*). Beni Selam has close relationship with the Nilotic Shilluk, where they intermarried in many places. Beni Selam claims that their ancestors buried deep in Southern Sudan since 1720, among their ancestors: Sheik Byr Abu Noah (nicknamed: owner of Pen and *loah* – a sophism board for writing Qu'anic verses) and Sheikh Sulieman Abu Daoud (nicknamed: stripped tiger and the honest host of people belongings). *Darih* – the burial tombs, for both sheikhs, seasonally renovated and decorated with flags and other *Semani* religious sect items. Cultural elements of Beni Selam well noticed in the Upper Nile State of Southern Sudan, and in their close relations to Shilluk people.

Many of Beni Selam are traders; they have large agricultural schemes in the Upper Nile State, before secession of South Sudan, which employ many Southerners during agriculture season.

Beni Selam tribe boarded in the north by Ahamda tribe and northwest by Jima'i tribes; to the west boarded by Awlad Himayd and Habbaniya of South Kordofan (Adil A. Mahmoud, 2006). To the east boarded by the White Nile. Awlad Himayd and Habbaniya are Baggara tribes, which represent the extension venue for Beni Selam to the rest of Baggara people of western Sudan.

Beni Selam tribe is among the most nomadic Baggara tribes; they spend about nine months in Southern Sudan and only about three months in Northern Sudan. Like all other Baggara, they own large herds of cattle, in addition to, considerably large herds of sheep, goats and camels. Staple food for the tribe includes dairy products, sorghum, millet, meat and others such as gathering of wild honey, hunting large games and fishing.

Beni Selam tribe divided into two main sections: *Mahboub* section and *Um Traif* section; the two sections encompass 15 subsections, which represent Beni Selam of the White Nile.

Beni Selam used to be under one local administration with other nomadic tribes on the White Nile (named Baggara of White Nile Local Administration) under *Nazir* Maki Asaker. However, later they split and establish their own administration under their first leader Omda Musa El Zein, who ruled the tribe for almost sixty years, survived by his son, Omda Nour El Din Musa El Zein.

Like other Baggara tribes, Beni Selam are courageous warriors. One of the excellent poems praising themselves says:

We are Selam and Seliem our father
We kill the largest game and take out its teeth
If we refused to pay tributes, the Turks could do nothing about us
Who we did not forcibly milk his milking cow?
Who we did not slaughter his largest bull?
When we take our spears, resemble heavy rain pours
Our javelins cases make noise like large crowd of birds' chirpings
We are well known among tribes, and we are dangerous if we come
We sacrifice our own kids to save other ones.

AWLAD HIMAYD:

Awlad Himayd tribe is part of the Baggara fraternity of Kordofan and Darfur. They speak Baggara Arabic dialect. Like any other Baggara tribes, they are Sunni Muslims. Awlad Himayd lives on the eastern parts of South Kordofan. MacMichael (1922), mentioned that their ancestors may have settled around Tekali Mountains, the eastern part of South Kordofan, at a time of the vast Guhayna movement and they reinforced by others of their kin, who have returned from the western countries, probably from present day Chad. They are nomadic Baggara people who share routes (sing. *morhal*, pl. *marahiil*) with the Halafa branch of the Hawazma, Kinana, Kwahla, and Habbaniya (this is a part of Habbaniya of Darfur settled in South Kordofan) tribes. They share the land with Tekali tribes of the Nuba Mountains and Shilluk of the White Nile. They are widely viewed among Baggara as courageous Baggara people; they are skilled hunters of elephants and game such as giraffes, antelopes, tiangs, and ostriches; at earlier times, they were known as extraordinary fighters of wild beasts such lions, tigers, wolves, and others. Stories about bravery of their ancestors reveal how they value bravery. One such story was that of a *faris* – a knight, called Ibrahim *Al Ghoum* – the name literally translated as Ibrahim *the Nation*. Ibrahim was the son of the legendary leader Nazir Didan of Awlad Himayd. Once upon time, Ibrahim sent his servant to carry his rope-bed in order to place it under a large, densely shaded tree, in a highly closed canopy jungle. Once the servant reached the tree, he found a lioness with her cubs; the lioness eye-balled him and he – the servant - promptly went back to inform his master. The Knight Ibrahim took the bed himself and went to the same tree. He and the lioness squarely eye-balled each other; immediately the lioness started to carry her cubs one at a time and moved away from the tree where Ibrahim *Al Ghoum* took refuge from sun heat. Such legendary stories, which reminiscent of Arabs tribal history, narrated by grandmothers and grandfathers to their grandsons with enormous passion and enthusiasm. Ibrahim was one of the legendary Baggara worriers. There were a large body of praise by *hakamat* (female poets) and *hadayiin* (male poets) written on his honor. The poems said during festivities, war times, leisure times, or tribal ceremonies. Because of their courage, Awlad Himayd nicknamed by Baggara as grey bees (*Nahala el ghibasha* in Arabic), the fiercest bees in South Kordofan. Their seasonal migration travel takes them as far as the Southern Sudan to meet with the Shilluk Nilotic tribe of the Upper Nile. Their inner southern nomadic area is part of the wilderness of South Kordofan, a dense, high savannah forestland. The majority of Awlad Himayd are pastoralists, and the rest are farmers, some of them are large agricultural schemes owners. In general, they grow all types of South Kordofan crops: sesame, sorghum, millets, okra, cotton, and groundnuts. They grow Gum Arabic and collect gums, and honey from the wilder of South Kordufan.

Awlad Himayd are great Baggara gardeners and orchards growers; Abu Jubeyha – their headquarter city, has more than one million fruitful Mango trees.

Early in the eighteen century, they entered the Nuba Mountains, at the time when King Nasir was at the reign of Tekali region. Since that time, Awlad Himayd have their home in South Kordofan, and their headquarter at Abu Jubiha city; they have a large presence in cities like Rashad, Abbasia, Tekali, Liri, Kalowgi, Talodi, Um Draba, near Tartar region, Abu Tilah and Kaka. They are present in almost all villages east of Tekali Mountains.

Awlad Himayd are descendant of Himayd (Himayd is a son of Heymat - one of the ancestors of Baggara), their grandfather gave birth to two sons: Shuab and Gadief. Shuab branch represents Shuabat subsection of Awlad Himayd, who lives in northern Kordofan together with Hamar to the point that they become as if a branch of Hamar tribe. Gadief, the other son of Himayd, gave birth to three sons: Ali, Ahmed and Aboud. Descendants of Ali called *Amoud* in the tribe of Awlad Himayd and the descendant of Ahmed called *Doufria*, while descendants of Aboud are living outside Sudan borders, probably in Chad. Each of *Amound* section and *Doufria* section has grown into ten subsections; these twenty subsections represent Awlad Himayd proper who live in South Kordofan today (excerpts from late Amir Abdelrahman Kambal). Their first paramount chief was Nazir El Alyan ca 1831 (*Nazir* is the highest tribal designation), and the eighth chief was their paramount chief Nazir Didan, who was one of the greatest Baggara chiefs in his era during Mahadism in 1881 (MacMichael, 1922). In 1932, Awlad Himayd created strong alliance with the King Nasir of Tekali. Because of that alliance, the Governor General of Sudan awarded Nazir Radi Kambal, the paramount chief of Awlad Himayd, rule over southern Tekali Mountain tribes, such as Kwahla, Kinana, Kalowgi, Liri, and Talodi, in addition to their own tribe of Awlad Himayd (Owen Sharif Gasim online resources). Chief Radi Kambal was trustee, loyal to, and strong alliance for King Nasir among the tribes of southern Tekali region; similarly, King Nasir of Tekali had enormous respect and admiration for Nazir Radi Kambal.

Similar to his relation with King Nasir, Chief Radi Kambal had strong ties with *Mek* (King) of Shilluk tribes on the Upper Nile - the Chief Kor Faviti; their relationship helped both to cultivate alongside each other, where Shilluk used Awlad Himayd experience in cultivating and tapping Gum Arabic trees. The relationship between Nazir Radi Kambal and Mek Kor Faviti had grown into strong alliance, and in 1944, Chief Kor had awarded half of Kaka area to Nazir Radi Kambal, where the later established one of his mansion, a court place and a mosque (from Amir Abdelrahman Kambal). Awlad Himayd had similar amicable relation with many of Nuba tribes such as Kalowgi, Talodi, Iiri and others, where they have ruled over these tribes for years under the era of King Nasir of Tekali. Similarly, Awlad Himayd amicably ruled over other Arabic tribes in the region such as Kinana and Kwahla tribes.

Awlad Himayd besieged twice during recent history by Turks, where they confiscated all their wealth and similarly during early Mahadism. However, the tribe recuperated and established its presence and rule over their land and joined the Mahadism in large numbers (Mac Michael 1922). They have some of the greatest commanders of Mahadism like Amir Younis wad Dikiem and Faris ez Zouma.

HAWAZMA:

As one of the largest Baggara Fraternity tribes, Hawazma are cattle herders who roam the area from the southern parts of North Kordofan to the southern borders of South Kordofan. Hawazma raise cattle, sheep and goats. However, unlike other Baggara, they stopped growing horses due to horses' disease in the area. Hawazma families also mostly own one or two male camels to carry their luggage. As a tribe, they are mostly occupying routes originating from El Obeid city of North Kordofan and running through South Kordofan. Hawazma main headquarter is El Hamadi town in the northern border of South Kordofan, along the national highway between El Obeid city and Diling city. El Hamadi city found just north of Dibebat town, which is a main train station in the line between Kowsti and Nyala. Hawazma have considerable presence in cities such as El Obeid, Kadugli, Diling, Abu Jubeyha, Rashad, El Abbassia, Talodi, Um Brambita and El Fayd Um Abdulla. All these cities and others represent part of *dar* El Hawazma (*dar* means land). Hawazma's *dar* engulfs South Kordofan and southern parts of North Kordofan, where Hawazma share the area with many other ethnic groups such as Nuba of the Nuba Moutains, and Bideria, Masabaat, Kinana and Felata of North Kordofan. Hawazma boarded to west by Missiriyya Zurug and to the east by Awlad Hymaid and Habbaniya tribes. At their southern boarders, they reach up to Lake Abbyad on the border between South Kordofan State of Northern Sudan and Unity State of Southern Sudan. On the northern border, Hawazma reach up to El Obeid city during their herding season where they have considerable, permanent presence in the city.

Hawazma have three main large divisions: 1. Abdel Aal, 2. Rawawga, and 3. Al Halfa divisions.

Geographically, Abdel Aal division lives on the northern part of

South Kordofan, around Diling city and up to El Obied city, with major concentration on El Goz area (*Mahaliet El Goz*); their headquarter is in El Hamadi city along El Obeid-Diling highway. Rawawga division lives on the middle of Nuba Mountains, mainly concentrated on east, southeast and south of Kadugli city at villages such as Buram, Um Dorain, Um Sirdibba, El Aheimer, with major concentration on Kadugli city, where their main headquarter located. Halfa division mainly lives on the eastern Nuba Moutains such as Rashad, Al Abassiya, Fad Um Abdalla, Um Brambita and others.

Hawazma tribe has many sub tribal divisions. At a very high level, these divisions are: (1) *Abdel Aal* branch, which includes: a. *Dar Salam* (which includes *Dar Bakhoteh* and *Dar Gawad*), b. *Dar Niy'elaye*, c. *Jima'iyya*, d. *Awlad Ab Baggar*, e. *Awlad Ghaboush*, and f. *Dar Beyti*. (2): *Rawawga* branch includes a. *Dar Jam'i*, b. *Awlad Nuba* and c. *Delamia*. (3): *Halfa* division includes: a. *Dar Ali*, b. *Dar Faid*, c. *El Asirra* d. *El Asirra Ba'shoum*, e. *Awlad Ghonaym*, and f. *El Togia*.

In his book, "Hawazma tribe", Ali S. Hamouda (2004) chartered 28 Hawazma tribes for the above subdivisions, including 71 sub tribal divisions, each sub tribal division called *surra* (the *surra* further divided in to kinships called "*khoshoum biyut*" sing. "*khasoum bayt*"), (see Cunnison, 1966)

Hawazma ventured and ultimately settled in South Kordofan since the Arabs tribes reached the region around early sixteenth century when Tekali Islamic Kingdom established ca. 1505, on the eastern mountains of the Nuba Mountains area of South Kordofan State. In about 1775, Hawazma permanently settled in South Kordofan. In 1791, Chief Tawir Abu Jarda of Rawawga branch of Hawazma born on the location of the present city of Kadugli – the provincial capital of South Kordofan State. Later, in 1800, Hawazma settled almost all the plains of Southern Kordofan and established amicable reciprocal relationships with the Nuba's *Meks* and tribes. In 1821, South Kordofan born Baggara son Tawir Abu Jarda became the paramount chief of Rawawga branch in South Kordofan; during his era, Helmi Basha, the Governor General of Kordofan, insulted him and he replied by killing many of his Turks servants in South Kordofan. In response to the killing of the Turks, Helmi Basha sent Lietenant Kambal Agha in 400 of his troops (locally called Bashbouzok – in Turkish *başıbozuk*, literally means 'damaged head' meaning foolish or disorderly), but they were defeated by the Nazir Tawir Abu Jarda and lieutenant Agha escaped. Eventually, Helmi Basha led his army by himself and killed Nazir Abu Jerda and his Rawawga branch of Hawazma dispersed in the Southern Mountains of

Buram, Korongo, Um Sirdibba and others, seeking refuge among their trusted Nuba alliances.

Historically, Hawazma had strong alliances with the Nuba people in the Nuba Mountains, to the points that many branches of Hawazma tribes acquired their names by annexing or suffixing the word "Nuba" to the branch name such as Awlad Nuba branch of Rawawga, Rawawga Um Sirda (*Um Sirda* is the name of one of the Nuba Mountains).

In 2010, and in reference to Hawazma-Nuba alliances, Hussien Adam Karshoum, a journalist, wrote the following oral story as a symbol of coexistence. In his narration, Kharshoum wrote; "My grandfather, Ibrahim, was a Mahadist Commondar, leading a column of hundred men called '*raas mia*' during Mahadism. When the British defeated the Mahadisn in Sudan, they sent a group of soldiers from Kadugli city to capture or kill the grandfather and his men. A fight erupted and embattled Ibrahim wounded and fell in a water stream seemed as if drowned. Assuming he was dead, the soldiers left the place. A Nuba knight, his name El Jamal (literally the Camel) from Shatt tribe found him still alive, carried him to the Shatt Mountain and brought a local herbal practitioner who medicated him for days until cured. El Jamal and his uncle Abu Digené went to Humra village looking for Ibrahim's kinships; they found his brother Arabi gathering an obituary for his death. El Jamal told them that Ibrahim was alive. Arabi and his relatives moved with El Jamal to Shatt Mountain, where they found Ibrahim alive and brought him home. Since then, an alliance established between Dar Jam'i branch of Hawazma and Nuba Shatt. On the summer of 2008, Ibrahim Adam celebrated his alliance with Nuba Shatt in El Humra village in large gathering." In the same article, Karshoum narrated another oral story about how was the name of the Mountain Korongo-Abdulla in the Nuba Mountains came into existence (Kornogo a name of a Shatt's Nuba worrier and Abdulla is a Baggara *faris* from Rawawga section of Hawazma). In that story, a wounded Abdulla carried by Korongo to the mountain of Korongo. Rawawga and Nuba Korongo established an alliance, which led to the renaming of the mountain to Korongo-Abdulla. Suliman (1999) cited three different agreements, which were signed between the Baggara and Nuba SPLM faction in the Nuba Mountains, these are: The Buram Agreement signed in February 1993; the Regifi Agreement signed on November 15, 1995; and the Kain Agreement signed in June 1996. All agreements led to easing of the embargo against the Nuba SPLM faction set by the Government of Sudan.

Oral history had shown that, Hawazma were tough and resolute fighters among themselves and with other fellow Baggara. Some of the major reasons of feudalism were occupying land or acquiring cattle of other clans. One of the legendary Hawazma knights was El Hassab El Nasiba (literally: Al Hassab *the Nightmare*) of Halfa branch of Hawazma. The *faris* Al Hassab fought many battles with Baggara's Awlad Himayd over acquiring the settlement of Abu Jubeyha area in South Kordofan, ultimately, the fight ended by sharing the area between Awlad Himayd and the Halfa branch of Hawazma. Knight El Hassab had no rivalry with the exception of the legendary knight Ibrahim *Al Ghoum* (Ibrahim *the Nation*) of Awlad Himayd. Abdulrahman Kambal, the late *Amir* of Awlad Himayd, said on his unpublished book "Awlad Himayd", once upon a time Ibrahim *Al Ghoum* disagreed with his own tribesmen said "any beard did not attended my father's era I will not listen to what it says". He left his tribesmen headlong. Al Hassab of Hawazma tribe and his men seized the moment and followed Ibrahim, where a dragging battle ensued. Eventually, Ibrahim killed by a trick made by El Hassab colliding him on a low hanging tree branch which El Hassab avoided by throwing himself off his horse while Ibrahim closely followed him and was unable to avoid the branch. Ibrahim severly fractured his head and fallen unconscious. In recognition of his bravery, El Hasab and his men buried Ibrahim in a place known as Waja Rimali near Lake Liya – a known place to Awald Himayd tribe. Similarly, Hawazma fought many battles with their kin Missiriyya on their west side. One of the most mesmerized battles named the battle of *"the Boabab of Vultures"* (locally called *Tabalidyat El Nousura*) on the northwest of Diling city, where many men killed from both sides, and the embattled fighters of both side extremely exhausted, and vultures started snatching flesh of the wounded and dead corpuses while the battle was raging. Eventually people raised Qur'an books on their lances and spears, to signal the end of the war, and to say, "Enough is enough". Among the great knights of Hawazma in that battle was a man named Ghaboush Tor El Nahal (the *Drone*) of Dar Bakhoteh branch and a man named Ma'touq Azrag of Awlad Ab Baggar branch. Hawazma were strong force during Mahadism; they were part of the conquering force besieged the Diling city, Al Obeid city and were a leading force in the attack and demise of Hicks Pasha forces on Shikan battle. They fought almost any battle agaist the British including Karari battle.

Through their transhumance movement, Hawazma in particular and Baggara of South Kordofan in general, know the area, terrain, ethnic groups, local tribes, tribal cultures, ecosystems, climate, vegetation, existence of risks and diseases, and water resources better than any other inhabitants of the region.

MISSIRIYYA:

Missiriyya (Synonyms: Messirya, Messiria, Missiriyya, Messiriyya) are a large branch of the Baggara fraternity of Kordofan and Darfur. Their language is the Baggara Sudanese Arabic; they are Sunni Muslims. Like all other Baggara tribes, Missiriyya raise cattle, sheep, goats, camels and horses. Staple food for the tribe includes dairy products, millet, sorghum, bulrush millet, meat and others such as fishing, gathering of wild honey. Historically, Missiriyya occupy West Kordofan (locally known as *Dar El Missiriyya*) and part of west Nuba Moutains, and they have considerable presence in Darfur, and significant presence in Chad. Among their well-known locations, which represent main headquarters are: Babanousa, El Muglad, Lagawa, El Mairam, Abyei, and Lake Kailak.

The main divisions of Missiriyya in Kordofan are Missiriyya Zurug (literally the name means *the dark ones*) and Missiriyya Humr (literally means *the red ones*). These names, *Zurug* and *Humr*, do not mean in any way that the *Zurug* are darker in skin color than *Humr*, but most likely, the names come from their ancestors' nicknames – Baggara are particularly fond of nicknames and no Baggara man found without having a nickname. According to Mac Michael (1967), the two divisions have become so distinct that the *Humr* have ceased to rate themselves Missiriyya. However, in Sudan today, still they called Missiriyya Humr and Missiriyya Zurug and still they acknowledge their common history and ancestry. The term *"Dar El Missiriyya"* means the land or location of the Missiriyya. In general, the *"Dar Al Missiriyya"* or their zones divided into three areas: Dar Al Missiriyya in West Kordofan in Sudan, Dar Al Missiriyya in Darfur in Sudan and Dar Al Missiriyya in Chad. Missiriyya in the three different zones separated for long times to the point that they have developed localized cultural and social differences. Missiriyya elders in Kordofan know the fact that Missiriyya of Darfur and Chad belong to the same tribe and they have similar sub tribal divisions and diversities. Dipping into Missiriyya of West Kordofan division will give a considerable insight of their divisions in Darfur and Chad.

The main divisions of Missiriyya further divided as follows:

Missiriyya Zurug – According to MacMichael, 1967 the *Messiria Zurug* have the following divisions: a. *El Ghazáya*, b. *Awlád Um Sálim*, c. *El Enenát*, d. *El Diráwi*, e. *Awlád Na'amán*, f. – *El Zurug*, and g. *Awlád Haybán*. Other sources replace *El Diráwi* subsection with the name *El*

Doru'a. Mubarak Mahmoud Farah (2011) eluted to the fact that subsections of a. *El Ghazáya*, b. *Awlád Um Sálim*, c. *Awlá Na'amán* and d. *Awlád Haybán* are all group in one section as *Alawneh*. Thus, Missiriyya Zurug subdivisions simplified into *Alawneh, El Enenát, El Doru'a* and *Zurug.*

Missiriyya Humr divided into two main sections: 1. *Ajaira* and 2. *Felaita* with further subdivisions according to Cunnison (1966) as follow: subsection of *Ajaira* divided into a. *Fayyarin*, a. *Awlád Kamil*, c. *Mezaghna*, d. *Fadliya*, e. *Menama*, and f. *Addal.* Similarly, subsection of *Felaita* divided into a. *Metanin*, b. *Ziyud*, c. *Awlád Serur*, d. *Jubarat* and e. *Salamat.*

Missiriyya, mostly, live around West Kordofan and western part of the Nuba Moutains, and their *dar* extends until the border zone between Sudan and Southern Sudan, specially the southern fringes of their nomadic zone – known as Abyei area.

Seasonally, Missiriyya migrate to the river Bahr Al Arab at Abyei and Lake Abbyad during the dry season, where they spend most of the year. Missiriyya Zurug lives on the east of *dar* el Missiriyya sharing the area with Nuba tribes and to their eastern borders found their kin Hawazma. On the west side, they bordered by Rizeigat tribe, with Missiriya Humr mostly lives on the western part of *dar* al Missiriyya. On the north, Missiriya bordered by *dar* Hamar with cities like Eidaya and Abu Zabad as their northern borders.

Missiriyya, Humr and Zurug, involved in some historical grazing disputes along their southern borders over grazing and water resources with the ethnic groups grazing the area. The traditional disputes intensified during the first Southern Guerrilla's wars called Anyanya 1. In 1964, a whole Missiriyya nomadic camp, around Lake Abyyad, massacred in a heinous human slaughter by Anyanya fighters; none were spared including children, elderly and brides; many abducted and women raped by the rebels. Missiriyya retaliated with a sequence of attacks targeting Southern villages, which culminated, in 1965, in the killing of many of Ngok Dinka members who were living in the town of Babanusa – a base homeland town for Missiriyya. Without any need for external interventions, Missiriyya and Ngok Dinka amicably resolved such isolated disputes and fighting. Since 1983, with renewed second civil war between the North and the South of Sudan, relationship between Missiriya and Ngok Dinka has taken different turns. Ngok Dink sided with South Sudan rebels while Missiriyya sided with Northern Sudan Government. The Abyei area became a contentious hallmark of the renewed civil wars.

Historically, Abyei area recognized by Northern Sudanese as part of *dar* al Missiriyya, yet, Ngok Dinka, who migrated to the area in ca. 1905, during British rule of Sudan, claims the area to be theirs. While Missiriyya are Baggara Arabs, Sunni Muslims and identify as Northerners, on the other hand, Ngok Dinka identifies as Southerners and Africans either Christians or Animists (with minor presence of Muslims). Missiriyya oral historians tell that, one of their ancestors named Sheikh Abu Nafisa his burial found far southern of present Abyei township, and he died around early seventies of the eighteen century. Henderson (cited by Mac Michael 1922), Mac Michael (1967), and Cunnison (1966 p. 3) all attest to the presence of Missiriyya in Abyei area in the eighteen century, around the year of ca. 1775. On the other hand, there is no conclusive history available for the nine Ngok Dinka chiefdoms on the area as seen from the chronology of events at that time. Being both nomads, Missiriyya and Dinka Ngok, coexist amicably for years and shared the area's grazing resources. However, an impasse created following the clear indication of eminent split of the country in 2011, into North and South, along 1956 borders, following the CPA (Comperhensive Peace Agreement) between North and South. On July 11, 2008, the Government of Sudan and the SPLA (Sudan People Liberation Army of the Southern Sudan) deposited an Arbitration Agreement with the PCA (The Permanent Court of Arbitration based in The Hague). A five member's arbitral tribunal constituted to decide the case, with the PCA acting as registry and providing administrative support. In 2009, the PCA redrew Abyei borders. Although all parties publically endorsed the ruling, however, on the ground, the impasse continued to exist. In July 9, 2011, South Sudan seceded from North Sudan but Abyei area remained a disputed area.

Historically, Abyei inhabited by Dajo and Shatt people before Missiriyya or Ngok Dinka migrated to the area. Ahmed A. Arbab (1998) a Dajo intellectual, said: "after the downfall of Dajo Kingdom in Darfur in the sixteenth century, they dispersed east, and west". According to the author, part of the Dajo migrated west, and established Dajo Kingdom in Chad. Ismail A. Abbaker (2005) also a Dajo intellectual, said: "Dajo who migrated eastward established their kingdom in present day Muglad area with their capital in an area called "*Atmour El Dandur*" east of Muglad city". Henderson (1932) said "The migration, which brought the Humr to their present homeland, said to have consisted also of the Messiriya, the Rizeygat, and the Hawazma, and, according to some versions, the Awlad Himayd and Habbaniya as well". Henderson continued to say, "The most commonly recounted tradition among the Humr is that they undertook the journey to evade the demands of Sultan of Wadai. When they reached the land called *Denga*, whose center was the place now known as the Muglad, they found pagan people called Dajo and Shatt in possession and drove them out. The Humr quarreled successively with the other Arab tribes that had accompanied them, battled them all away, and retained the place for themselves. It has since remained headquarter (the *dar*) of the tribe" (cited by Cunnison 1966 p.6). Many resources showed that, southern borders of Dajo Kingdom extended from Kafia Kingi region in South Darfur State to Lake Abbyad in South Kordofan State. Dajo people own account stated that a people named Jur Chol (other names Jo-Lou or Lou) in Bahr El Ghazal were on the Southern part within the Dajo Kingdom, and their name in Dinka language means "the Arab" (see Awad Abbaker Ismail, Sudan National Archives online resources, published on Feb. 03, 2011).

Literature from Southern Sudan indicated that Jur Chol wondered for some time before settling, and indeed, Dinka gave the name to Jur chol. However, Collins (1971) said, "The word Jur Chol means an individual or a group without a permanent location. That indicates that that tribe got its name upon entering the region of Bahr Al Ghazal, moving to the west, east and south of that region. It was also said that, that the name given to the tribe by the Dinka because of the latter's ignorance of the language of the Jur Chol and its continuous movement in Bahr Al Ghazal." Nowadays, the most northern land of Jur chol people is Aweil district of Bahr El Ghazal State of Southern Sudan – Aweil district borders Abyei on its southern border. In essence, the story of the presence of Jur chol as part of Dajo Kingdom suggest that, once the Kingdom downfall, it split into two parts; the southern part became what nowadays known as land of Jur chol and the northern part – including Abyei - as the *dar* of Missiriyya.

Looking at Abyei issue from Southerners perspective, the head of SPLM Veterans for Truth in Diaspora in London, Atem Mabior (2007) stated that, "Historically, we have established according to our research, the present Abyei belonged to the Dajo tribe, which is now dispersed into Southern Kordofan, Southern Darfur and Eastern Upper Nile. The cause of this dispersion might have been caused by Ngok Dinka incursion into Abyei area. Claims by Ngok Dinka and the Messiriyya to the area are all false and unsubstantiated. We know that the Messiriyya and the Dinka were in Abyei by the 17th and 18th Centuries. Can they tell us that this area was unoccupied when they invaded it?" Indeed, The Missiriyya said that the Dajo people occupied the area, while Ngok Dinka does not recognize this fact in their oral history, which indicates that they never met chronologically. Mabior missed the point in two of his arguments: when he said Ngok Dink might disperse the Dajo, which is historically untrue. There is no mutual written history or oral history for both Ngok Dinka and Dajo to support this claim; on the other hand, there is a wealth of evidence and oral history by both Missiriyya and Dajo to support the claim that Dajo was driven away by Missiriyya and their kin Arab tribes. Mabior (2007) further stated "in 1905 for administrative reasons or otherwise, decided that Abyei be annexed to South Kordofan from Bahr Al Ghazal. The most important point we want to put through is that this decision was not unilaterally made but was made through the free will of the then leadership of the Ngok Dinka under the paramount chief Late Deng Majok. So far we know that Abyei was not the original homeland of both the Ngok Dinka and the Messiriyya and that the British colonial administration annexed it to Southern Kordofan in 1905 with the consent of the Ngok Dinka." Possible question is where is the original homeland of the Ngok Dinka? When they migrated to Abyei area? It is known from when and from where the Missiriyya came to the area. Clearly, Mabior questioned the claims of Ngok Dinka to Abyei area.

Francis Deng, a scholar from Abyei and grandson of the leaders of Ngok Dinka chiefdom said, "Oral history and historical documents date the first contact of the Ngok Dinka and their Northern counterparts, the Humr Arabs, at 1745" (Francis, 2009). Francis (2009) further said "the Ngok Dinka trace their history through their paramount leaders, of whom they count eleven generations. Kwoldit, ninth in the line, is the leader who believed to have settled the area around 1745". Francis continued to say, "Biong's Arob established peace with the Humr Arabs by entering into a brotherhood pact with his Arab counterpart. This fostered cordial relations between their respective peoples. During the Mahist revolution 1882-1885, Arob went to pay his allegiance to its Islamic leader, Mohamed Ahmed, the Mahdi ..." As opposing to Mabior, Francis Deng made no reference to where Ngok Dinka came from to their present location in Abyei.

Amin Hamid Zainelabidin (2009) argued that, taking the known timeline when Arob met Al Madi as a cornerstone point in history, and moving back or forth through all known Ngok Dinka leaders to Kwoldit, does not match up to 1745 chronologically. Zainelabidin (2009) further said "inferring events from time of Ali Abu Groun, who led Missiriyya between 1823 - 1835, assuming average age of 50 years for a person and a period of 20 years as a period for each Ngok Dinka chief rule over the tribe, the chronology for Dinka chiefs, while ruling should be: Aweil Jok: 1815 - 1823, Kwoldit: 1823 – 1843, Alor: 1843 – 1863,

Biong: 1863 – 1881, Arob Biong: 1881 -1905, Kwol Arob 1905 – 1944".
This critical, historical analysis indicates that Ngok Dinka migrated to
Abyei, between 1823 – 1843 time span, during Kwoldit period, when he
was in the reign of the tribe. Another evidence comes from the
Explorer Ferdinand Werne, who visited South Sudan between 1840 –
1841 said, "the only group of Dinka who were not subject to Nuer
attack in the mid of eighteen century was Ngok Dinka, who were living
south of Sobat river; they left them alone, because they lack cattle and
their area was poor ...". Zainelabidin (2009) said, "The original land for
Ngok Dinka is on the northern border of Giraffe River, and they only
migrated from there because of floods and Nuer attacks". Zainelabidin
further said, "Paul Howell said, in this regard, it is difficult to determine
a conclusive date about when Ngok Dinka migrated, but according to
the analysis of generations' ages among Nuer and according to the
explorers' maps, it is likely Nuer attack on Giraffee River happened on
the nineteenth century". The Missiriyya were on the region since ca.
1775, which is way back before history traces the migration of Ngok
Dinka to Abyei area. Clearly, Nuer and Dajo (and probably Jur Chol)
history and oral history strongly support Missiriyya position.

Apart from Abyei empasse, Missiriyya tribe is on the greatest Baggara
tribes. Historically, they were the first to adopt Mahadism among the
Baggara people and played key role in mobilizing Baggara against the
British rule and their defeat in Sudan.

RIZEIGAT:

Rizeigat (Synonyms: Rizeigat, Rizegat, Rezeigat or Rizayqat) are one
of the largest and most powerful tribes of Baggara fraternity of Sudan.
Musa A. AL Hassan (1995) said about them: "they are the wealthiest, the
most numerous, and the strongest of all Baggara tribes". Ahmed A.
Adam (1997) said "Rizeigat nicknamed by Baggara tribes as sons of
Rizeig, a handful of earth –in Arabic: "*iyyal Rizeig hiyn al turab*"; this
means they are numerous. Rizeigat tribe is, probably, the largest tribe in
Sudan and they are the largest in Darfur. Flint and De Waal (2008) said,
"The Rizeigat are the largest and most powerful of all the Arab tribes of
Darfur". They are Sunni Muslim. They speak Baggara Sudanese Arabic
dialect. Da'ein city, along Kosti-Nyla railway line, is the main
headquarter for Rizeigat. Their main staple diet includes dairy products,
millet, sorghum, bulrush millets, and meat. During hunger and famine
times, they can harvest wild rice (called *kariab*). Unlike other Baggara,
Rizeigat are equally nomadic cattle herders as well as camel growers.

Accordingly, they are divided into two groups according to animals' types they rear: (1): the Abbala (camel-herding) Rizeigat who mostly inhabit northern Darfur and Chad, and (2): the Baggara (cattle-herders) who inhabit southeast, south and southwest of Darfur. Flint and De Waal (2008) said, "South of Jebel Marra, the Arabs took to herding cattle – becoming known as Baggara, or cattle-people – while those in the north remained as Abbala or camelmen".

Rizeigat of southern Darfur, - the Baggara - bordered from south by Bahr El Arab – at about 26 km (~ 16 miles) south of Bahr El Arab; on the eastern side, bordered by Dar Hamar and Missiriyya; on the north bordered by Al Bigo, Dajo and Birgid (Al Hassan 1995), and on the west, bordered by Habbaniya tribe. Rizeigat of northern Darfur – the Abbala - bordered from north by Libya; on the eastern side, bordered by Ziyadia, Berti, and Meidoub; on the western side, bordered by Fur and Katinga tribes (Adam 1997).

Rizeigat divided into several large clans (tribes), notably: Mahamid, Mahariya and Nawaiba. The same divisions exist within Abbala of northern Darfur as well as within Baggara of southern Darfur. Because of the large extension of Rizeigat *Hakura* (*hakura* means land in Darfur), each clan owns its land and chiefdom. Rizeigat Baggara, of southern Darfur, headquarters as follow: Nawaiba, of southern Darfur, headquarter is at El Fardous area (earlier known as *Adhan Al Humar* – literally means *Donkey's ear*). Headquarter of Mahamid, of southern Darfur, is at Assalaya (previously known as: Ghemalaya literally means: *Little Lice*). Maharia, of southern Darfur, headquarter is at Abu Jabra area. Kutum locality is the headquarter of northern Rizeigat - the Abbala ones. Rizeigat also lives in a large number in west Darfur. According to Ahmed A. Adam (1997), both Mahamid and Maharia have *omodiyyas* in El Jinana, the capital city of west Darfur. Similarly, Mahamid and Nawabia have their *omodiyyas* in Wadi Saleh Township of west Darfur. In addition to the divisions of Rizeigat, also, there are other tribes, which all considered Rizeigat due to their blood kinship with Rizeigat proper such as Eteifat, Ereigat, Zibilat and Shattia. Furthermore, Rizeigat have strong alliances with tribes such as Beni Hussien and Awlad Rashid, and many sections of other tribes joined ranks in Rizeigat tribe such as section of Zaghawa in north Darfur, Eishayshat and Gidyania and others.

Historically, Rizeigat power as a tribe was demonstrated by creating strong alliances with others. Once, such an alliance created of all sons of Al Juneid, the common ancestor of all of the Baggara Arab tribes in west Sudan, during early settlement of Arabic tribes in Darfur, against

King Sharango of Beni Khuzam tribe. Rizeigat were able to put an alliance of all the three divisions of the Attawa, Awlad Heymat and Awlad Rashid together to defeat King Shrango. The legend has it "a man named Arigi Fanni had a female camel called *Al Angha'a*. The camel Al *Angha'a* had a lot of milk that instantaneously poured by itself. The owner, Arigi put a large animal's skin (called *sien*) around the *Al Angha'a* waist to collect the pouring milk. The *Angha'a* had strange habit of grazing during night times instead of day times. Once upon a time, it went and grazed on the tree where King Sharango used to hold his court. The King noticed his court's tree shade became sparse and ordered his servants to hunt down the animal which was grazing on his court's tree. The guards stayed night long until the *Al Angha'a* came about the place and took her in custody until delivered to the King in the morning. The King saw her perfuse milk, and he asked his servants to hide the camel away for his own use and not let anybody to know where it was hidden. In the morning, Arigi, the owner, came about following the footprints of his camel until the place of the King court. He went to the King to ask him to allow him to fetch his camel in his land but the King refused. Arigi knew from a story of two Khuzam women who quarreled each other and one of them insulted the other by saying: you are stealers of Arigi camel; the women secretly went up to Arigi family and told them that the King was hiding the camel. Arigi repeated his request and continued his appearance in front of the King requesting to give him back his camel. The King refused and ordered him not to come back again. Angered by the King refusal, Arigi insulted the King. He said, "the moving is Atia; the settled is Heymat, and the drum trumpeted daylong belongs to Rashid Al Walad. A loser Khuzami King will not be able to take my camel by force"; this saying was a blunt threatening to the King by Arigi, telling him that he will collect all of Attawa, Heymat and Rashid sons together to get his camel back. At that point, the King took pride on his power, and replied back to Arigi: "go and collect all those of Al Juneid (who include all Baggara tribes), and Magnud (who includes all Abbala tribes), all these just like a herd of sheep which will not be able to face off with a lion". Of course, the lion was the King himself.

Arigi went back to his family quarter, took a camel and branded it with a sign of a cry under its eyes. Arigi rode the camel for months roaming Baggara and Abballa tribes and their kin sons of Rashid Al walad, telling them how the Khuzami King abducted by force his camel – the *Angha'a*. Arigi said strong legendary poems praising *Al Angha'a* whenever he went. Arigi story strongly resonate across Baggara and

Abbala alike.

Eventually a battle broke between King Sharango against all the Attawa, Heymat and Rashid sons. The King defeated, and many of his tribe Khuzam killed and the rest dispersed. A woman, from Khuzma tribe, hunted down the camel *Al Angha'a*. When Arigi found his camel dead, he stepped off his camel and narrated one of best and most mesmerized poem in Baggara traditional oral history, in praise of '*Al Angha'a* and other poems demeaning Khuzam tribe and insulting King Sharango".

The battle although seemed mythological, but it has a strong presence in all of the Baggara tribes oral stories, with some variation of the narration, and of the name of the battle. Hassan M. H. Al Nahla (1993) has written a book called "*Fanni Camel*" narrating the story, and he concluded that the battle was the one which led to the demise of Beni Khuzam Kingdom in Chad. Similarly, Ali H. Saleh (2004) narrated the stored on his book "*The Hawazma Tribe*", from the Hawazma side point of the oral history.

Rizeigat, also, exerted strong leadership among Baggara tribes and matchless power when allied themselves with the Mahadism Revolution against the British, and when they reversed course against the Mahadism during Khalifa ibn Abdullahi El Ta'ishi tenure after the death of Imam Al Mahadi – founder of the revolution. Musa A. Al Hassan (1995), book titled "*Darfur Political History*" could well be argued that it is mainly a history of Rizeigat during the Mahadism time. Similarly, Rizeigat, especially Baggara Rizeigat, showed strong restraining power during Sudan civil war (1983 – 2005) mostly by refusing to join the tribal or ethnic wars.

Rizeigat known for their passion for horse riding, poems writing especially war's poems (called *heday*). Rizeigat women singers (called *hakamat*) are strong galvanizing force during war times.

HABBANIYA:

Habbaniya or Habbania tribe is part of the Baggara Fraternity of Darfur and Kordofan region. Like other Baggara, they are Sunni Muslim and speak Baggara Arabic dialect. Unlike other Baggara, Habbaniya are the least nomadic Baggara tribe. Habbaniya tribe occupies two distantly separated lands: one in South Darfur and the other one in east of South Kordofan – the Eastern Mountains. No one knows why the tribe split into two groups, with each group composes of the full divisions of the parent Habbaniya tribe. In any case and for whatever reason may be, one part departed and moved far away – for about 500 miles or more to settle in east South Kordofan, while the rest of their kin stayed in South Darfur. The two groups still intermarriage and visit each other. Mac Michael (1922) said, at the time when he wrote his book, it was about eight generations passed since the tribe split. According to Thesaurus dictionary, generation's gap is a difference in values and attitudes between one generation and another, especially between young people and their parents. Taking Mac Michael (1922) words of eight generations and estimating the generation gap of between 16 - 20 years for Baggara, it is likely that, Habbaniya moved between years of ca. 1762 – 1796. Looking at events shaping Baggara life, migration, and movements during that time span, one fact stands out that is the migration of Baggara eastward to evade the demands of Sultan of Wadi. Henderson (1932) said: "The migration, which brought the Humr to their present homeland, said to have consisted also of the Messiriya, the Rizeygat, and the Hawazma, and, according to some versions, the Awlad Himayd and Habbaniya as well". Henderson continued to say: "The most commonly recounted tradition among the Humr is that they undertook the journey to evade the demands of Sultan of Wadai". It is likely that Habbaniya who settled in east South Kordofan are the ones returning from Chad with other Baggara tribes, who temporarily settled with their kin in south Darfur and moved eastward to distance themselves from the long arm of Sultan of Wadai.

Like all other Baggara tribes, Habbaniya are Sunni Muslims, and they speak the characteristics Baggara Sudanese Arabic dialect with slight but notable pronunciation variations in Baggara Arabic dialect such as most of the Baggara say for the question: Where are you going? They say "*wein mashi*" but Habbaniya say: "*yein mashi*", replacing "w" letter with "y" letter, similarly, Habbaniya say for women "ayein" instead of the common Baggara dialect "awein".

According to Musa Al Mubarak Alhassn (1995), Habbaniya divided into two main sections: 1. *Tara* and 2. *Sowt*. The *Sowt* section further divided into two subsections: a. *Shaba* and b. *Shaboun* with each section further divided into further subsections. The *Tara* section divided into two main subsections: a. *Rayafa* and b. *Shaboul* with each section further divided into further subsections. In total, Habbaniya have around twenty-seven subsections; all of them represent the main body of the Habbaniya tribe.

In Darfur, Habbaniya *hakura* located south of the Magdoumia (headquarter of Dafur Sultans) – the current Nyala township, starting from its north tip at Darisa Gate "in Arabic: *Bawabat Darisah*) in the area known as Guriedeh and extending south until Bahr Al Arab at a place called Al Hijirat area. East border shared with Rizeigat at town of Um Suntta (Suntah), and on the south side, there their borders end at Kafia Kingi Township – on the border of South Sudan. On the west, Habbaniya bordered by Central Africa Republic and to the northwest bordered by Ta'aish tribe.

Habbaniya headquarter is Buram city (nicknamed: *Alkalaka Um Al Diyar* – literally the mother of all lands). Habbaniya have anecdotal sayings about *Alkalaka* say "the lands are only three – the sacred Mecca which glorified by God, the Green Tunisia and the free land of *Al Kalaka*". They say, also, "*Al Kalaka* has *wiz* (ducks), a drum when trumpeted say diz diz, and a large *waral* 'monitor' which is never *yafiz* 'never runs away'". From such sayings, one can glimpse a feeling of love and deep sentiment of Habbaniya to their homeland.

The landscape of Habbaniya *hakura* in South Darfur is one of the most picturesque areas in south Darfur region, just like Beni Halba *hakura* landscapes. The area has many seasonal streams, and valleys, which impede movements during the rainy season. In the area, there are large water pools and lakes, such as Lake *Kindy* (called *Buhirat Kindy*), which attracts abundance of migratory birds. The area has high rainfall up to 800 mm per annum, highly rich soils and abundance of underground water and water aquifers. The largest Baggara Aquifer "in Arabic: *hawd al Baggara*" passes right under Habbaniya *hakura*. The area is home to many beautiful birds such as cranes (called *gharnoug*), wild pigeons, wild ducks and rare gazelles; it is home to the second largest protected area in Sudan – the *Radoum* Natural Park, which comes second after the *Dinder* Natural Park on eastern Sudan. The area also has large reserves of petroleum, gas and precious metals.

In the eastern part of South Kordofan, Habbaniya live south Of Um Ruwaba area between Rahad (Rahad Ab Dkana) and Shurkala, on the eastern Mountains of South Kordofan. Their locations include Shurkala city, which is headquarter of Habbaniya and other tribes. Shurkala lies on the southern banks of Abu Habil valley, surrounded by a large number of villages to the east and to the west of the city where Habbaniya live. At Shurkala, people name Abu Habil valley as the Nile '*El Nil*' and they nickname Shurkala city as the hand of the Nile' "in Arabic *Iyd el nil*'. Abu Habil valley at Shurkala, especially during the rainy season, floods in a large area, creating a large body of water pool, where large *sunt* trees (*Acacia nilotica*) grow in dense canopies. However, Abu Habil valley represents significant impeding factor for the movement of people living in Shurkala. During the rainy season, it is quite difficult to cross to the nearby Um Ruwaba city, although the distance is only about one hour driving. Shurkala is an old city – older than Um Ruwada city, which established in 1911, and it is an old trading center, where traders visit it from as far places as Omdurman, Kowsti and El Obeid. Sheikh Mustafa Al Amin, a well-known wealthy man, maintains his shop at Shurkala until recently.

BENI HALBA:

Beni Halba is one of the Baggara fraternity tribes located in Darfur region of west Sudan. The main headquarter for Beni Halba is *'Idd al Fursan'* town in Darfur – literally, the town name means *"the Wells of Knights* or *the Wells of Horsemen"* indicatives of Beni Halba bravery and courage.

Beni Halba *dar* (term *dar* means land also called *hakura* in Darfur) located in south Western Darfur State; it is situated in one of the most picturesque landscape of southwest of Marra Mountains, characterized by an abundance of rains and seasonally flowing valleys and creeks, which impede movement during rainy seasons. Seasonal water pools draw a large crowd of birds, such as sandpipers, wild ducks and pigeons. Beni Halba *hakura* also rests on one of the largest natural water aquifers – the Baggara Aquifer. Their *hakura* (land) located east of Garcela region, north of *dar* Al Ta'aisha tribe, southwest of Marra Mountains – one of the most beautiful landmark in the region. During their seasonal transhumance journey, they meet with Ta'aisha and Salamat tribes on Reheid Al Berdi – the capital city of Ta'aisha tribe on their southern borders. They intermingle with Falata tribe at Tulus city to the north, and they meet with Habbaniya at Buram city – headquarter of Habbaniya tribe on their east side; also on the east side they meet with Rizeigat tribe at El Da'ein city – the headquarter of Rizeigat. They mix along their transhumance journey with many other tribes in many cities towns and villages in the area such as Shattaya area, Kas, Zalingy – the two later cities are large Fur tribe centers. They meet most of Baggara sections and tribes on Um Labasa cattle market, which is the largest cattle market in Darfur State. They pass south across villages of Madi, Mainjo, Flindogy El Sarakh, and along the banks of Bulbul seasonal stream across the First Crossing at Bulbul Dalalat Angra and the Second Crossing at Bulbul Timbsko. Across these villages, Beni Halba intermingles with a large number of African tribes, such as Fur, Dajo, Gimer, Sinar, and Burno, where they intermarried. Beni Halba has considerable presence in northeast of Nyala city, the provincial capital of South Darfur State. On the northeast of Nyala, they intermingle with Berti, Birgid, Mima, Zaghawa, Ziyadia, Tungur and Meidoub tribes (Ahmed A. Adam, 1997).

Beni Halba along with Habbaniya, Rizeigat, and Ta'aisha tribes represent Baggara fraternity tribes in Darfur, and these tribes together represent the largest portion of Arabs in the region. Like all other Baggara, Beni Halba raise cattle, sheep, goats, camels and horses. They are gifted horse riders and superb cavalries (called locally *fursan* in Arabic) in the region. They breed one of the best Arabian horses; they have annual derby gathering in Nyala city, which draws a large crowd of spectators. Staple food for the tribe includes dairy products, millet, meat and others such as gathering of wild honey.

Historically, Beni Halba *fursan* played key roles during Mahadism and current Sudan civil wars since 1983 – 2005. As a result, the Beni Halba district town of *Idd al Ghanam* ("*Well of Goats*") renamed Idd al Fursan ("*Wells of Fursan*").

Beni Halba has two large sections: *Jabir* and *Jubara*. The headquarter of *Jabir* section is on Abi Hamra, while Jubara section headquarter at Reheid El Birdi, with cities as Kubbum and Kabsa as principal centers for Jubara section. *Jabir* section further divided into four subsections: a. *Jam'an*, b. *Ali*, c. *Ghyath* and d. *Labeid* sections. *Jubara* section divided, also, into four subsections: a. *Jozour*, b. *Alwan*, c. *Musa* and d. *Rajab*.

In 1990, Beni Halba of all sections congregated in a large congregation of the tribe. One of the critical outcomes of the congregation was to unite the two branches of the tribe into one body. The body called *Nazaria* or *Amara of Beni Halba*, and to be ruled by a single paramount chief selected in rotation between the two large subsections. The congregation agreed that if the *amir* – the paramount chief selected from *Jabir* section then his deputy should be selected from *Jubara* subsection and vice versa.

In all, Beni Halba are excellent Baggara people with extraordinary traditions of horse breeding and mastering, which enable them to be one of most superb horse riders in Sudan today and through its history.

TA'AISHA:

Ta'aisha is one of the leading Baggara tribes. One of the great ruler of Sudan named Khalifa Abdullahi ibn Mohamed Al Ta'aishi, from Ta'aisha tribe. Khalifa was the ruler of Sudan for almost thirteen years during Mahadism, after the death of Imam Mohamed Ahmed Al Mahadi

– founder of Mahadism Revolution against the British. In 1885, Al Mahadi and his Deputy (Khalifa) Abdullahi Al Ta'aishi defeated the British and expelled them from all over the Sudan. Since then, Ta'aisha tribe remained one of the most respected tribes in Sudan in general and among Baggara in particular.

As Beni Selam is the most eastern Baggara tribe, Ta'aisha is the most western Baggara tribe. Ta'aisha tribe is part of the Baggara Fraternity of Darfur and Kordofan. Like any other Baggara tribe, they are Sunni Muslims and speak Baggara Sudanese Arabic dialect.

Ta'aisha land (*hakura*) located on the southwest of Darfur region, between latitudes 10 - 11° N. Headquarter of Ta'aisha located at 'Reheid El Berdi', a beautiful city and among the most mesmerized cities of Western Sudan in all over Sudan. The picturesque landscape of 'Reheid El Berdi' city inspired many singers and artists to include the name of the city in their artistic works. One of the best songs sung by the famous singer Saleh ibn Al Badia has part of it says "and a glimpse of beauty from the beautiful Reheid El Berdi". Singer Saleh ibn Al Badia's song, which includes 'Reheid Al Berdi' city, is a sensational song for Sudanese people, just like the famous 'America, the Beautiful' lyrics by Ray Charles. The high fascination of Sudanese artists by the landscape of 'Al Reheid' city is a testament to the beauty of the natural habitat and landscape of Ta'aisha land.

Ta'aisha *hakura* bordered from the north by Beni Halba *hakura*, where *Shaib* Valley represents their natural border. It extends toward the south until the Republic of Central Africa, where Ta'aisha crosses its border during their summer seasonal journey. On the east side, they bordered by Habbaniya tribe, while on the west side, bordered by Chad. During their summer seasonal migration, Ta'aisha cross Chad border, just like what they do in the case of the Republic of Central Africa, to graze their animals. In addition to Ta'aisha *hakura* in southwest of Darfur, they migrated in large numbers during Mahadism and settled in Omdurman city – where Omdurman's residential areas such as Hay Al Umara, Al Shouhada, and Al Malazimiin were all established by Ta'aisha people, who migrated from southwest of Darfur – *dar* Al Ta'aisha.

Musa A. Al Hassan (1995) and Adil A. Mahmoud (2006) mentioned that Ta'aisha tribe has two main sections: (1): *Al Uroj* and (2): *Al Gulada*. *Al Uroj* section has thirteen subsections, while *Al Gulada* section has twelve subsections with many minor subsections within *Jubarat* section and *Um Raida* section. Farah Aisa Mohamed (1982) believed that Ta'aisha tribe is best represented by three large sections that correspond to the descendants of Ahmed T'aish – the ancestor for the tribe, as: (1):

43

Awlad Marzoug, (2): *Awlad Sirag* (*Al Jubarat*) and (3): *Awlad Hadloul*. Adil A. Mahmoud (2006) further noted that, Ta'aisha not only included descendants of Ahmed T'aish, but also the descendants of his brothers such as *Awlad Amer* and *Awlad Sa'id*, and descendants of Ahmed T'aish daughters such as *Awlad Salama*.

Ta'aisha, like all other Baggara, raises cattle, sheep, goats, camels and horses. They are gifted horse riders – just as Beni Halba does and superb cavalries (called locally *fursan*) in the region. They breed a large number of Arabian horses; probably, they participate in the annual derby gathering in Nyala city, which draws a large crowd of spectators. Staple food for the tribe includes dairy products, bulrush millets, millets, sorghum, meat and others such as gathering of wild honey.

During Mahadism, Ta'aisha were a galvanizing force. They led Baggara tribes to adopt the Mahadism, and to migrate, in large numbers, to settle in Omdurman, the capital city of Mahadism, which nowadays part of Khartoum triads: Omdurman, Khartoum and Khartoum Bahri, which make up the capital city of Sudan – the Khartoum city.

Among the most noted leaders of the tribe were Khalifa Abdullahi Al Ta'aishi - the head of the State and many amirs such as *Amir* Yagoup (the brother of Khalifa Adullahi), *Amir* Mahmoud wad Ahmed, *Amir* Younis wad El Dikeim, *Amir* Ahmed Fadeel, *Amir* Al Khateem Musa and many more who fought famous battles across time span of the Mahadism era..

4 BAGGARA: CHARACTER, FAMILY, SOCIAL SYSTEMS AND TRADITIONS

BAGGARA CHARACTER:

Baggara people have graceful, slim physical statues; their skin color ranges from light brown to dark colors (at the end of this chapter, plates included to familiarize readers with Baggara faces, statues, dress and costumes, and some ways of their life). MacMichael (1922) described them as being lithe in color. Explorers to the region motioned that they have far better mental capabilities, keen intelligence and humor than any other tribes around them; they have a passion for life and collective life style.

Baggara nomads are beautiful people. In his book, "*The Cross Roads of Africa*", Bashir M. Saeed said, "The Baggara are wonderful people – friendly, honest, healthy, clean, clever, brave and proud", cited by Ali H. Saleh (2004). Along Shari River in West Africa, Baggara nicknamed "*Shuwa*", which means the "*Beautiful ones*", by the Kanuri people. Owens (1993) wrote that. "The Kanuri word '*šewa*' which is pronounced '*shuwa*' meaning beautiful". Sudanese people admire the Baggara beauty in the Sudanese society. One of a well-known, renowned Sudanese singer, Ibrahim Musa Abba , has one of his sensational songs called '*al Ajako*' dedicated to the Baggara beauty, saying: "see how Baggara are beautiful between the city of *Talodi* to the city of *Bara* while dancing *nogara*". Both cities are falling on the far ends of Baggara grazing ranges – *Talodi* to the south, while *Bara* to the north. *Nogara* dancing is characteristic of Baggara people across their ranges. When Baggara trumpet *nogara* drum, everyone jumps into the dance including girls, boys, young men, and women, in a particularly elegant way. At the end of the *nogara* dance, a dance's queen selected and adorned in a remarkably similar way in many respects to the selection of beauty queens on the West. The song, *al Ajako*, also sung by two women singers – they named '*Thounayee el Naggam*' they have added a new flavor to the song saying, "From *Nuhud*

45

to *Bara* and from *el Da'ein* to *Nyala* see the beautiful Baggara how they dance *nogara*"; *el Da'ein* city is one of the Baggara major headquarters in Sudan.

Baggara character is substantially shaped by what they do for a living. Nomadism and transhumance are profoundly shaping how exterior world sees Baggara people and leading to the emergence of Baggara culture – *Baggarism*, a vastly debated topic among anthropologists (further see Adil A. Mahmoud 2006, on the emergence of Baggara culture). Ian Cunnison (1966) eluted to the fact that the environment and ecosystem shed a positive light on the Baggara life. Many cited that Baggara are powerful warriors and courageous fighters. Since their migration to Sudan, Baggara have been formidable forces shaping Sudan history. They greatly shaped and determined the fate of many events. Some even resented Baggara saying their only character is courage. El Tunisi (1803, p. 139), when visited Darfur shed some light on the Baggara character, saying: "In the southeast of Darfur are living the Arabs nomads like Missiriyya Humr, Rizeigat and Fulan and each tribe of these Arabs nomads has numerous population; they rear cattle, horses and have furniture. Most of them possess animal wealth, and they do not like sedentary life, but they move about to whatever place where there is pasture and water". El Tunisi (1803 p. 140) said "Darfur sultans take tributes from Arabs nomads every year, but Missiriyya Humr and Rizeigat do not pay any healthy cattle, and sultan's emissary cannot force them and if he dares he get killed and sultan do nothing about them". El Tunisi (1803 p. 140) further said, "It comes to my knowledge that Rizeigat of Baggara tribes reject to pay tribute to Sultan Tirab of Darfur. He prepared an army but defeated, then the Sultan followed them with his army by himself, but the Baggara retreated to swampy areas and dealt a severe blow to Sultan Tirab army, which took heavy casualties".

Baggara are curious people and always have the sincere desire to be well aware and acquainted with their environment. Curiosity always seen in their inquisitive demeanors, and in many instances, a Baggara man can get up and walks to a moving caravan to inquire its people about where are they going? Where are they coming from? What are they carrying? He is curiously sniffing for any unusual signs in their eyes.

Baggara women add different characteristics to Baggara character with their characteristic lower lips sticking, their feverous passion for bravery songs keeping Baggara men on their toes during war or fighting.

When Baggara go to cities or move to urban areas, they can easily blend into the general Sudanese society and acquire a life of city dwellers. Baggara are easy goers; they can easily establish friendships with others and engage in a constructive dialogue even on just a road encounters.

One of their prominent characteristics, is their collective life style where all people in a camp gather in a single spot and share their food dishes – all the time, in a place they called *dara*. Baggara are amicable people and only turn to fighting mode if someone messes with their women or wealth.

THEIR APPEARANCE AND COSTUMES:

With the exception of old men who wear a white gown, Baggara are colorful in their dress and costume.

Men wear a white gown called *jallabiyya* or *jebba*, white pants (called *sirwal ab tika*, sort of pajamas), a head cap called *taggia*, large white turbans called *eema* and a locally made leather shoes called *markoub*. Always men of all ages carry knives, which worn on the biceps of the left arm and hidden in a decorated leather covering; they carry sticks, spears, swords, stout spears or automatic weaponry (see Plates at the end of this Chapter). Women wear a dress called *foustan*, and cover their bodies with Indian Sari locally called *taubes*. Young men wear eye-catching, colored flashy shirts, shorts, pants, beads, necklaces, and bracelets. Young women wear *foustan* and mostly cover their head with colorful scarfs. During festivals and dancing, Baggara girls, mostly, go without covering themselves in *taubes*, and usually carry lump of ornate mixture of perfumes on their braided hairs. The ornate material called *tarbal* or *tarbalul*, it is a conglomeration of many aromatic plants and other constituents: *basil, sandalwood, mahlab (Prunus mahaleb)*, bees wax, animal's fat, perfumes and other local herbs – all affixed directly on the braided hair endings during hair braiding. *Tarbalul* has exceptionally strong aroma and can be smelled from far a distance, which alert to the presence of a young Baggara girl. Young Baggara girls known for their extremely rich and colorful dresses; they always tend to fashion their dress in inextricably exotic way.

Men in their late ages usually cleanly shave their heads, while young Baggara usually style their hair in Afro-style or close haircuts. Women of all ages braided their hairs and wear silver and golden jewelries.

THEIR DOMES:

Baggara build rounded domes called domes, which are semi-circular or half-globular domes, from trees' branches and saplings. Usually, branches and saplings inserted in holes arranged in a circular fashion and bended inwards and tied together; smaller saplings and branches fill spaces between branches. Baggara cover their domes with mats made from doum palms (*Hyphaene thebaica*). Women are responsible for building of the domes.

In general, Baggara have two types of domes: summer domes and rainy season domes. Summer domes built the in a similar way as the rainy season domes, but it is thatched with grasses instead of mats in case of the rainy season domes. Summer domes are larger and more spacious than rainy season domes (for detailed description of Baggara's domes see Chapter: Baggara Material Culture).

THEIR FOOD AND CUISINES:

Baggara staple food is milk and milk products, sorghum, and millets. In most cases, they make porridge of sorghum or millets and add to it fresh milk or a sauce made of milk and other ingredients.

Like other Sudanese cuisine, food in the Baggara cuisine has almost inextricable aroma and taste. The flavor is vibrant with little spices but sometimes drift into spicy side, featuring milk and fresh meat products like *roub* (sour milk sauce), *mite'eina* (milk sauce), *um halibayn* (milk porridge), *tagalia* (dried meat sauce), *jidad makashin* (chicken or meat marinated in dried, peeled and fried onions). Baggara also enjoy drinking milk, sour milk and *nasia* (skimmed milk added to it little water and lots of sugar) and others. Flavored tea in cinnamon or mint is one of the signatures of their hospitality. Exotic dishes are also common such as *kamonia* (mixture of raw liver, lungs and spleen treated in a sauce of sliced onions mixed in groundnut or sesame paste, hot spices and chilies). Even more exotic, however, exceptionally delicious is *kawari* (animal feet juicy soup, where feet eaten, and their soup treated with taste of lemon and hot chilies). One of the most intriguing dishes is *abu ghazii*, which is meat into which they add the digested content of the small intestine during cooking). Baggara also eat *Kawal* dish, which seem exotic even to the general masses of Sudanese. *Cassia obtusifolia or* synonym *Senna obtusifolia* (*kawal* plant) green leaves are fermented into closed jars, to produce highly protein-rich cakes called "*kawal*", which has a sharp, pungent smell slewing into somehow nasty smell spice. The *kawal* cake is sun dried and powdered before use as spice. It is usually splashed in food just like black pepper with similar color – dirty dark color. Eating *kawal* as spice is addictive; once used to it, one cannot help but to add the smelly spice to one's food. *Kawal* originally not made by Baggara but by African tribes; however, Baggara buy it and use it to the point that it becomes like a Baggara dish.

Baggara also cook and eat as part of their cuisine the general Sudanese dishes such as *mahishi* (tomatoes, squash, and eggplant stuffed with ground beef with rice). Baggara also drink sweet juice such as lemon juice or Roselle juice (called karkadé juice). Kardadé juice comes from *Hibiscus sabdariffa* flower.

In Sudan, it is well understood that there are no recipe books – popular meals simply are handed down through generations, constantly evolving and improving. Baggara cuisine perfectly fit into a lost haven category even within Sudanese cuisine.

THEIR RELIGIOUS BELIEFS:

Baggara are Sunni Muslims, and many of them follow some religious sects such as Ansar sect in Sudan. Barbara Michael (1996) wrote "the Baggara are Muslims, and they observe the Five Pillars of Islam: the declaration of faith, the five daily prayers, almsgiving, fasting, and the pilgrimage to Mecca. Many Baggara men and some women, manage to make the pilgrimage to Mecca". Baggara eat '*halal*' meat, which usually done by slaughtering animals by a competent Muslim religious man; the animal slaughtering done by laying the animal down on its left shoulder facing Mecca direction and by saying: 'in the name of Allah, the Great' – (in Arabic: *b'ism Alah wa Allahu akbar*). If the animal not slaughtered in this way, it considered not '*halal*' and thrown. During eating, everyone has to say '*In the name of Allah*' before taking any bite from the food, and when everyone fishes eating says '*al hamdullah*', means thanks God.

Muslims in general have two main religious celebrations: after finishing fasting of Ramadan and one after Hajj (pilgrimage) – in the later case it is must for Haj person or any abled person to slaughter a horned lamb.

THEIR ARTS:

Baggara people have different forms of arts, range from their colorful fashions and dresses to coloring of their bulls' horns. Women do a lot of artwork such as leatherworks, hand embroidery, tanning of clothes, and much more. Women and grandmothers also do artworks of gourds, colorful food dish coverings (*toubag*), and air-blowers (*hababat*) and making of colorful mats (*broosh*) either made from the date palm (*Phoenix dactylifera*) or doum palm (*Hyphaene thebaica*) leaves. Young women also make highly decorated beads, bracelets, necklaces, wrist wearing, and hair styling and decorations.

Baggara men also sew decorated head caps from silk (*tawagi, tagia*) and handkerchiefs and make decorated knives and swords coverings. In addition, Baggara men make elaborately decorated horses' saddles, camels' saddles and donkeys' saddles. Young men make decorated beads, bracelets and necklaces.

BAGGARA FAMILY:

Baggara family, like any other Sudanese family, composes of immediate members and extended family members. The immediate family usually comprises of a husband, a wife, children, grandmothers and grandfathers, and in many occasions grandchildren for the family and servants who rear their cows, sheep and goats. The extended family composes of uncles and cousins including distant relationships. Baggara family is large; women are exhaustively giving birth to the last pitch of their biological capacities. A family size per one mother as large as fourteen or fifteen children is usual in Baggara society. A man in some instances could have more than thirty children, ultimately they span into a complete village or a branch of a whole tribe. Since Baggara are Muslims, they marry up to four wives at a time. Women for the same man build their domes next to each other in the Baggara camp. Grown sons always built their domes to the right of their mothers' domes until they close a circle, making a camp.

ROLES AND RESPONSIBILITIES IN THE FAMILY:

MEN:

In a Baggara family, men are the guardian of families and their wealth. Building, protection, and maintenance of herds are responsibilities of men. Baggara never grow cattle for economic reasons but purely for prestige. The prestige always bestowed upon the head of the families – the men. Men play a dominant role in Baggara family; they care about the overall well-being of families and their protection. Men serve as traditional judges, jurors, social workers for collecting blood's money, consultants, tax collectors and the alike. In many occasions, they form extra-judiciary councils to resolve an eminent crisis between or within tribes. They declare war and peace between and within tribes. They also cultivate farms to maintain the grains for the family or they sell animals to bring the family needs along with women.

Since Baggara society is a patriarchal society, men rule and espouse all members in the families; they, always, issue advice, commands, orders and directions to all other whom they should follow-in the orders.

YOUNG MEN:

Young men, from about 15 years to just before adolescence, are responsible for the overall day-to-day animal's caring and control of activities: they direct cowboys where to find desirable pasture, dig up wells, castrate male animals, pouch for next available grazing areas, and maintain animals' head count. Young men are the fighters against thievery, and they are the warriors and protective force of the tribes (locally called: *fursan*). They carry weapons of all sorts including semi-automatic calibers and machine guns.

One of young men roles is to serve as reconnaissance team during migration. A trusted young man (sometimes two or more young men) always sent by elders or a head of the Baggara camp to do reconnaissance survey and to see the new place where the camp should move next. The man will look for signs of nutritional grazing ranges including plants types, desirable grasses, disease if any, water locations and quality, soil types and condition, presence or absence of mud, harmful flies and presence of wars, enemies etc.

Young men usually receive orders from their elder men, and they give orders to boys, cowboys, women and young women.

BOYS:

Boys from unusually young ages up to 14 years old, and servants of all ages - usually named cowboys - carry day to day work: such as looking after herds day long, watering, giving animal's salt and maintaining animal's hygiene: by removing ticks, smocking away flies, cleaning wounds, removing thorns and clay from animals' hoofs. They are also responsible - together with young men - for taming and castration of young oxen, young sheep and goats. They carry milking of animals alongside women. They grow dogs for the family to protect animals or to use them for hunting, and care for them. Cowboys also designate exceptional care for bulls - sharpen their horns or decorate them. During family movement, boys are responsible for catching chicken and packing it in chicken coops (locally called *gufas*, sing. *gafas*) made grandfathers. They bring firewood and cook for a group when the cattle quartered away from families. Boys are the hardworking elements of Baggara families; they entrusted with all day in and day out herding activities. In addition, they have to listen to orders from other members of the families. Mostly they are the least cared about; they wear weary clothes and shoes (see Plate 16); they sleep on the ground if a guest comes and takes their place. Usually they not allowed to eat hand by hand with the elders or young men; they have to serve while others are eating; they will eat whatever leftover they find.

WOMEN:

Women are responsible for caring of kids and aging grandparents, and building of family quarters. They are responsible for cooking for family members, milking the cows together with the cowboys, dairy products' marketing, obtaining family needs from local markets, fetching water and firewood for family daily use, making of mats, and training of their daughters to be future wives. They do girls circumcision, act as midwives to carry all stages of babies' delivery, do facial scaring, hair-braiding, lips sticking, collect wild fruits, berries, rhizomes and wild okra, and exchange milk: with grains, groundnuts, sesame and other exchangeable products. Baggara women are remarkably well known for their capacity to exchange goods. Women also create leather workings to beautify their domes or to build decorative artifacts to show off during journeying from one place to another.

Women are singers to boost up morale for war – they praise the braves and belittle the cowards. They serve as referees and morale boosters for girls and young women during dancing.

YOUNG UNWED WOMEN:

Young unwed women and recently married women but not yet moved to their husband's quarters - carry all their mothers' duties to the point that they free them from any immediate responsibilities in the dome. Once this happen, young women move to other roles, such as preparation of wedding utensils for the recently married and unwed young women in the family.

GIRLS:

Little girls burdened as in the case of cowboys. They assist their mothers in cooking, water and firewood fetching, elders caring, domekeeping, and sibling's upbringing. Young girls if they have no boys' siblings in the family, they rear cattle, sheep and goats just like young cowboys do, in this case, they shift from girls roles in the dome to mostly animals caring roles.

GRANDPARENTS:

It is tempting to think that old Baggara grandfathers and grandmothers are just sitting around in the family quarter doing nothing or waiting for help. Such impression is false. Baggara's grandparents have unbelievably rich tradition of telling their grandchildren of Baggara's mythological stories of monsters, historical Baggara's bravery stories, recalling unusual events or wars and many more. They are the traditional historians of Baggara's societies; they are knowledgeable about tribal and family genealogy and history. They have wisdoms in pinpointing causes and effects of, and reading or judging the current events in Baggara societies and their future consequences.

Grandfathers also make ropes from trees' bark, or leaves, for all sorts of usage in the Baggara family, along with boys who get directions from grandfathers where to go and collect the barks, or leaves. In addition, they prepare water-carrying utensils from animals' skin (called *girab* or *si'en*), and they help to care for young animals kids.

Grandmothers have distinctive seductive babies' lullaby and rituals; they know how to massage the young borns and how to feed them or when to give them smoke bath; they know what trees barks, leaves or fruit to use for babies stomachache and aliments. In addition, they feed the new delivered women, and they care for them during the first two months for their delivery. They tan leather, make clay pots, work calabashes to hold milk.

Baggara grandparents are productive members in the family unless they are too old, and in such a case, they become too a burden for the family.

BAGGARA CAMPS:

Baggara camps (locally called *furgan*, sing. *farig*) represent higher order of Baggara family; usually the camp composes of one or more of Baggara families, mostly relatives, moving together during transhumance as one unit; in this way the camp represents an extended family. Although each family within the camp has its own daily routines, the camp has separate activities that span the families' roles or add another layer of roles and responsibilities. Men and young men are the principal actors at the camps level; they assume guardianship of the camps. A leader of the camp usually is the eldest of the active men. In the absence of such leader, the one who follow in age will assume the role of camp leader. All people in the camp succumb to his guidance and control. The leader directs the camp when to move from one place to another; he resolves disputes on behalf of camp or represents them in any social event with other camps. Mostly at camp level, there is a sense of shared responsibility among men in the camp; all men in the camp assume some unofficial responsibilities whenever they find themselves in a situation where there is no one else.

Although the camp is comparable to the family, yet families in the camp maybe distant relatives or even coming from very different tribes; this sense of loosely coherent group makes the camp like a village.

The way domes arranged in a *farig* (camps) projects strong sense of Baggara culture of solidarity and communal way of life. All domes in the camp open inward making a circle. Co-wives build their domes next to each other, with every new wife builds her dome on the left of the wife just married before her. Young men build their domes to the right of their mother's dome with the youngest married next to his mother's dome while the eldest married boy further away. Sometimes the camp composes of multiple smaller camps of kinship group (called *surra*). In many cases, the availability of water and grazing resources dictate size of the camp or number of camps in the area.

BAGGARA SOCIAL SYSTEMS AND TRADITIONS:

BAGGARA COURT SYSTEM:

It is not unusual to see under a large baobab tree a Baggara chief convened his court far away from cities in the wilderness of Baggara zones. It is not unusual to see a man kneeled down in front of the court with legs shackled and hands tied, and he bitterly lashed on his back. The man might be at hard to the point he is coo-cooingly weaning for mercy. A crowd of spectators might gather to witness the execution of court. They might be amused or agitated to see a fallen man in the hands of Baggara court system. Such a scene is usual and repeatable across Baggara zones of Sudan, from the White Nile on their east border to farthest point – Um Dafoug - to the west on south Darfur border with the Republic of Central Africa Darfur

Historically, Baggara court system shown strong presence among Baggara tribes, and in many occasions leads to strong ruling even in capital cases that ultimately upheld by a higher court circuit. The head of the system is the *amir*, who is the head of his tribe. In many cases, each Baggara tribe has one *amara*, which is the legal designation at the level of *amir*. Previous name of *amir* is *nazir*, still today well-recognized title by all Baggara tribes and *nazir* presides over the nazara of his tribe. Sometimes, there might be more than one *amir* per tribe, for example, Missiriyya Humr tribe of Baggara has two *amirs* – one for the branch of *Ajaira* and another for the branch of Felaita, and hence there are two *amaras*. *Amir* serves as supervisory body of his subordinates. The subordinates called *omad* (sing. *omda*). Each *omda* presides over his *omodiyya* – the official title of this post in the Baggara social system. The *omad* carry most of the cases, but if the case is complex it might require the *amir* attention or to be passed to the official country's court system. *Sheikh* is ruling over his immediate relatives called *surra*, but elements from other *surras* may join one sheikh making a large *mashiykha* – the official designation of this post in the Baggara social system. *Sheikhs* burdened by tax collection, bringing members' issues to the attention of the *omda* and they mediate on issues or crimes that do require court.

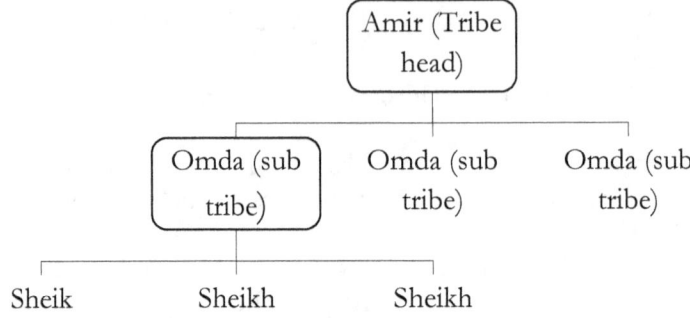

Figure 3: Baggara Court System official designation chart.

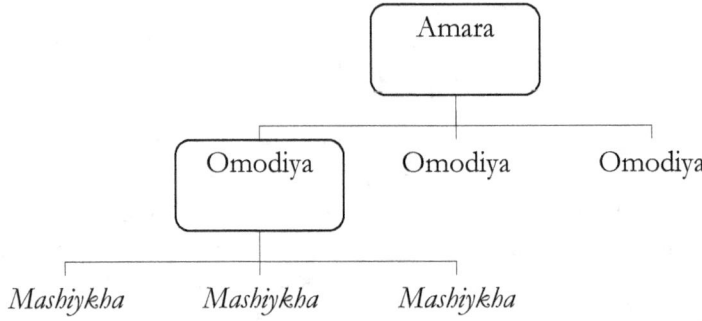

Figure 4: Baggara Tribal System organizational chart.

Amirs, *omad* and *mashiykh* (sing. *Sheikh*) are old men, or at their mid-ages; mostly they are men of prominent statues and great wisdom, well-dressed in large gourmets – called *jalabia* or *jebbah*, long and wide ground-brooding boogies – *sirwals*, a large turban –*eema* on their heads, underneath it piercing head-caps – *taggias* and large cashmere shawls around their shoulders. Their dresses are reminiscent of the historical stylish Arabian princes or Iberia's black Moors.

During the court session, men of all ages and social status can attend, they can chat, but with lower voices - occasionally, they argue loudly, in this case, the police of court – a normal person designated as police of the court, intervenes to silence group and maintains order; but all men keenly listen when the court in session. Court members dress gently in all the *choirs* - just as the *amir*, *omda* or *sheikh* might do. Cache of swards, spears, and sticks always seen piled at a tree stem near the court place. Baggara admires dressing when they are in festivities or when they visit marketplaces or convene in court. They walk in a scolding imperial or gladiator fashion full of prides even in the court place.

The court could be held for any reason and in any place – whether in an open space, makeshift dome, under a tree or anywhere else. Although there is an official clerk, who takes notes, yet there is no one else than the clerk maybe literate to read or to write; members knew their rules, and their court system by heart and they abide by it. It is a no-plea, no-appeal court. One has to pay his penalty. There is no higher court or lower court than the *omda* court within the Baggara social system, except the state official court, where a person can go and file an official appeal against the *omda* ruling. On Baggara court system, there are no written laws and there are no written documentations for courts – absolutely nothing for referencing; just the *omda* and his members come in empty handed and convene their court. If one proved guilty, he has to bear the consequence, or to pay his dues before he can appeal to the state's official judge. Mostly, the *amir* holds only occasional court for special purposes such as ruling on death cases, collecting bloodmoney or ruling between omad, and sheiks.

During the court session, attendees sit quietly: no movement, no side talks and no laughter. Jurors (members of the court) sit next to the *omda*. Once they asked they deliberate among themselves, and they announce their decision, such as guilty! Then the next step is to begin to execute the ruling – usually, either by asking for money or cattle in order to pay for the crimes, or lashing of a person; however, occasionally they send people to prisons. If it is blood court, the court asks for sixty-one heads of cattle be shared by all men of the tribes including the courts' men. None of the men ruling in the court might have studied law, and no one might have informal law training either. They could have gained their law experience by virtue of their respectful characters or wisdom they gained when grown older. It is a traditional court. The only presumed law is the customary law. The only essence of the law is the Samaritan law, where each court member contributes his own wisdom. With all shortcomings, the Baggara court system is a powerful court system, with considerable dignity, honor, respect and abiding ruling.

AJAWEED COUNCILING SYSTEM:

Counciling system in Baggara societies called *Ajaweed* Council; it is a traditional counseling mechanism; it existed for centuries as Baggara tribes' social counciling system to resolve feuding issues. Usually, *Ajweed* council causally formed to solve certain conflict. It is known under different other names such as council of elders or mediators. Charlotte

Hulley defined the council as a reconciliation council of elders. Hulley stated, "The council arbitrates the society at a family level, household level, clan level and ethnic group level. It is, therefore, an essential reconciliation process at the grassroots level". The council members bring conflicting parties together and deliberate over the issue for a long period of time in order to reach a fair settlement or a compromise, which is acceptable to conflicting parties.

Usually Baggara council members selected based on the merit of their moral characters. Council members are trustworthy men of extraordinary wisdom and superb life experience; they have nice manners, and possess unwavering commitment to justice, and righteousness deeds. Always, the making of the council is causal. Whenever there is an issue, some men select known honourable members as council, and conflicting parties accept their mediations. In other cases, a tribe congregation might select the council members, to mediate in high profile cases, such as fighting between different tribes.

Through Baggara history, *Ajaweed* council served truly noble cause for solving complex intertribal conflicts, and it continues to serve. Hulley stated "there are three key elements that require focus [of Ajaweed] when thinking about rebuilding of society that has been affected by violence. It is within the concepts of truth, mercy and justice that the bridge from violence to peace can be found" The guidelines or spirit of *Ajaweed* council follows Hulley descriptions of the three concepts above as follow: truth means acknowledgements, transparency, and revelation. Mercy means acceptance, forgiveness, support, compassion, healing and reconciliation. Justice means equality, restitution, rights, and responsibilty. Peace means harmony, unity, wellbeing, security and respect.

Ajaweed Council as a conflict handling mechanism entails the following core elements presented by Hulley:

a) Honest acknowledgment of the harm each party has inflicted on the other,
b) Sincere regret and remorse for the harm done,
c) Readiness to apologise for a role in inflicting the harm,
d) Readiness of the conflicting parties to 'let go' of anger and bitterness caused by the conflict and the harm,
e) Commitment by the offender not to repeat the harm,
f) Sincere effort to redress past grievances that caused the conflict and compensate the damage caused to the extent possible, and
g) Entering into a new mutually enriching relationship.

Ajaweed Council is one of best-known social system among Baggara and other tribes.

SABARA SOCIAL SYSTEM:

The *Sabara* means referees. This social system mainly deals with games, festivities and on other times deals with loss and grievances. As in case of football or soccer ball, which require referees, so do Baggara festivities and dance. Referees council usually coordinates competition between different tribes, control the events and mediate if any issue broke during the festivities.

Each tribe has known Sabara members who join other peers from other tribes to organize festivities. *Sabara* also watch over wrestling competitors. If one wrestler breaks the law of competition, *Sabara* will punish him or remove him from the competition. As there are men referees, there are women referees called (*sabariat*) who mediate on women dance, organize the girls during the dance and fix to them their hairs or decoration if missed up. In addition, women referees collect money awarded to women dancers. During marriages, also they collect money and keep it for common good.

MANADEEB SOCIAL SYSTEM:

The *Manadeeb* means delegates. Baggara have one of the finest delegation systems, where responsibility of taking certain action delegated to a certain group called *Manadeeb*, especially during feudalism between different tribes or clans.

Usually the Manadeeb considered subsystem to Ajaweed council system; in analogy to the judicial system, Ajaweed represents judiciary branch of the system (judges, jurors, and lawyers), while Manadeeb represents like a police force in the judicial system. They do things like a collection of blood money or gathering money from members to pay a loss of body parts etc. Usually, *Ajaweed* members instruct them to put a ruling of *Ajaweed* into effect. If an offender refuses to give a required amount of money, to surrender an unlawfully possessed wealth or items to *Manadeeb*, the offender referred back to *Ajaweed* to mediate. If Ajaweed reach an impasse with the defendant, they order the plaintiff to move his case to the country legal court system.

COMPENSATION SOCIAL SYSTEMS:

Baggara have three types of compensation systems:
a) *Diya* is the Blood Compensation money.
b) *Aoud* is the Compensation for loss of properties, possions or wealth due to accident or theft.
c) *Aourf* is an agreed upon ruling for a crime such as murder or an accident such as burning of a home, a thieft of a herd etc.

In case of death, the ruling called *diya* if the *Ajaweed* Council succeeded to resolve the issue before reaching the country judicial system. Thus, *aourf* and *diya* can be used interchangeably. There are two *aourfs* for *diya* – one for within a tribe and another for between tribes. The bloodmoney amount within a tribe might not be the same as between the tribes. Tables 1, 2, and 3 are some examples from Baggara *diya* within Missiriyya and Hawazma tribes and between Missiriyya and other tribes. *Aoud* considered when someone looses his herd due to theft or loss of his property due to fires and the alike. In this case, Baggara will collect the full amount and give it back to the person who suffered the loss.

The way the *diya* distributed among members of the tribes depends on what called sons of a man (*awlad al rajl*). Sons of one man constitute one group, and one of them should pay their part of the *Diya*, in the next occasion, another one of them will pay, until they loop again. If a man died, his children will pay a separate *diya* apart of their uncles, who continue to pay as a single group. If all brothers died, the sons of each one of them constitute separate diya paying group (they called *awald roujal*).

In almost all cases, *diya* paid in cattle heads. Most of the Baggara tribes pay 60 heads for the family of the deceased and one bull for Ajaweed as feast. The relatives of the offender person called *rukba* and usually they pay one sixth of the total number, which is about six heads. The rest will be distributed among the tribe members. Body parts have different values, for example, the right eye is half of total *diya*; the left eye is third of the *diya*; fingers of the right hand are more expensive that their corresponding of the left hand; index finger is more expensive than other fingers within one hand. Injury is paid in money. Loss of fertility such that a crime led to castration of a man, paid as a full price of the total *diya*. A woman's *diya* is half of a man *diya*. An unborn baby boy his *diya* is paid as full man's *diya* and, an unborn baby girl her *diya* is paid as full woman's *diya*.

Diya and *aourf* are complex social system but well-establish and known by all elders of the tribes.

Aourf can also take slightly different meaning to mean customary law. If two tribes were feuding, Baggara apply a ruling (*aourf*) called *saff* to separate them and distance them from each other to quell them. Sometimes, Baggara have strange *aourf*, for example regarding donkies, if someone kills a donkey or many donkies by accident, he has to pay the fine by himself alone without help from the tribe. If someone hired one's donkey and burdened the donkey until died, he pays no fine – for the reason that the donkey entitled to die under it is burden. Baggara do not buy or sell dogs. If someone alien comes and sold Baggara's dogs or puppies to other people, Baggara receive no compensations for their sold dogs, nor are they entitled for any money.

Table 1: Mubarak Mahoumd Farah (2011): Diya for murdur within Missiriyya tribes:

Age of a Cow	Gender	heads
First time calfing cows (*bikr*)	Females and a male	12
4 years old cows (*rubaiya* or *rabai'a*)	Female and a male	12
3 years old cows (*tania* and *tani*)	Females and a male	12
More than 2 years old and less than 3 (*jada'a* or *jada'*)	Females and a male	12
More than 1 year old (madmouna or madmoun)	Females and a male	12
Total		60 heads

Table 2: Mubarak Mahoumd Farah (2011): Diya between Missiriyya and other tribes:

tribes	Number to be paid in heads
Missiriyya and Rizeigat	70 heads
Missiriyya and and Dinka	30 heads
Missiriyya and Hawazma	60 heads
Missiriyya and Hamar	60 heads
Missiriyya and Nuba	30 heads

Table 3: Ali Hamouda Saleh (2004): Diya for murdur within Hawazma Abdel Aal branch:

Number and Age of a Cows	Number to be paid in heads
9 Second times calfing cows (*Um thany*) + 1 male of same age	10
9 First time calfing cows (*bikr*) + 1 male of same age	10
9 *rubaiya* + 1 *raba'a* (4 years old)	10
9 *tania* + 1 *tani* (3years old)	10
9 *jada'a* + 1 *jada'* (more than 2 years old and less than 3)	10
9 madmouna + 1 madmoun (more than 1 year old))	10
1 male bull (6 years old) for Ajaweed to feast	1
Total	61 heads

PARDONING (*FARYSH*) SOCIAL SYSTEM:

The *Farysh* Social system is pardoning someone or giving him something for the sake that pardoned person will forgo one in the future for similar deeds. Let us say, if someone's cattle break into another one farm, the farm owner may pardon the cattle owner hoping that the cattle owner will forgo him or his relatives if their cattle break into his farm in the future. However, if some pardoned someone, and the pardoned person does not forgo the person if a similar incident happens, the pardoner will request compensation for his earlier pardon.

The *farysh* goes even into cases of injuries, loss of body parts and others.

BARAMKA SOCIAL SYSTEM:

The *Baramka* Social System is an honorable system among Baggara tribes and its members. The *Baramka* constitute a lunatic constellation of men and women from different Baggara clans forming associations or clubs for ceremonial tea drinking (Cunnison (1966). *Baramka* sing praising songs in honor of a gentle man or a woman, who has done noble deeds, and sing disapproval songs for demonizing an unworthy man. The epic of *Baramka* social system is tea tradition, where they have strong abiding rules for how to drink tea, how to handle it and how to cook it – any abuse of tea is punishable. In their traditions, society divided into two groups: the good, benevolent, giving and caring group and the other group: the evil ones, who do not drink tea or honor tea traditions, they are cheap, mischievous and cowardly. The first group composes of the *Baramka* - the gentles (in their vocabulary called *hourafa*, sing. *harif*). The other group is the *Kamakla* (sing. *Kamkali*) group – these are the dishonorable thugs.

Baramka social system is an informal social group, within which *Baramka* (sing. *Barmaki* or *harif*) forms informal courts which rules on affairs that matter to them. Their ruling is only abiding to *Baramka* members, yet they have their own way of forcing anyone of Baggara people to abide by its ruling. *Kamakla* – the thugs, rarely attend the *Baramka* court, and for most of the times, *Baramka* do not allow them to attend – for reasons that *Kamakla* are dishonorable and cannot be honored by attending *Baramka* tea drinking gatherings. *Kamkali*, if invited for the *Baramka* court, he could refuse or could get up and walk away without permission or simply deny the ruling. The *Baramka* would not remain idle or helpless; they immediately categorize such a person as *Kamkali* – a thug or a mean of the meanest. The *Kamkali* remains all his life mean and dishonorable – thug. Unless he abides by the *Baramka* ruling, no one greets him, talk to him, or celebrates with him. He will remain lonely all his life - his friends should desert him and his wife be asked unofficially by *Baramka* to divorce him – just to belittle or to demonize him. He should not be honored with tea drink; he can only be given *asseida* – the porridge; and he will not be welcomed in any public gathering, nor no one will dare or allowed by others to attend his happy occasions. *Kamkali* is a thug; he will remain like a lonely pungent crap, a deserted useless junk, an untouchable creature, an alien, or a trash person of no value. He will face strong social rejection and condemnation. The *Baramka* orchestrate a complete embargo-styled social exclusion against the *Kamakla* for the reasons that these thugs do not honor the traditions that matter to them. The gregarious *Baramka's* behavior promote moral character, righteousness in behavior, comedy in daily life and preserve the Baggara way of life from degradation.

For Baggara people and specially the *Baramka*, tea is the single most cherished drink. One can honor a guest with nothing but tea. Nothing equates with tea. Tea's poetry is a signature of *Baramka* people. The honorable *Baramka* uphold tea traditions honorably, make poems to praise men and women respecting the traditions; the worst crime in the eyes of *Baramka* is to violate tea traditions – mishandling the cup of tea, cooking it on fire flame instead of charcoal, snoring in the cup of tea, not drinking tea and not honoring *Baramka* with tea. Tea's traditions enclave long lists of etiquette of handling and respecting tea.

The honorable *Baramka* can rule that someone be beaten upto forty lashes for violating tea traditions, and he should show remorse from his reprehensible act or he will bear the consequences of branding him as lifelong *Kamkali* - dishonorable. Anyone who labeled as *Kamkali* he bore a new nickname by prefixing or suffixing his name with the word *Kamkali*. No one should call him without saying *Kamkali* before or after his name; violators would be prosecuted and beaten up for not obeying the ruling. *Baramka* social system represents one of the fine social orders in the Baggara society.

MARRIAGE IN A BAGGARA FAMILY:

Baggara are polygamous and patrilineal. They marry once, twice, thrice or quadruple according to Islamic Sharia Laws. It is acceptable by religion to marry up to four co-wives; however, it is forbidden by religion to marry more than four women at the same time. It is acceptable as a religious practice to divorce and rejoin the same ex-wife up to three times, but after that, the ex-wife has to marry another man before she can return to her ex-husband. Her marriage from another man should not be made up as an excuse to return to her ex-husband. Men and women marry at young ages as soon as they reach adulthood. Married teenage mothers and fathers are common phenomena. Yet old men can marry young women even when they are at old ages. In general, Baggara could be categorized in the lower side of polygamous practice - mostly with one or two co-wives.

Marriages are mostly family arranged and occurred within close relatives. First cousins are the most preferred (Cunnison 1966). However, distant marriages are also possible. Dowry paid in cows' heads and money.

Baggara have rich marriage traditions, which entail almost a week of dancing and celebrations (Biraima Adam, 2013). The bride moves into her husband quarter after fourteen days after the wedding celebrations end. Baggara celebrate marriages by slaughtering oxen for feasting and bringing a lot of golden rings and items to the bride. The groom's father award at least one female cow or a bull to the bride's mother. The dowry is given directly to the bride's mother; and she can spend the money on celebration or may buy food items or clothes for her daughter. Mostly, the bride's mother keeps the cows or uses the money to cows and keeps them as wealth.

BAGGARA SOCIAL NORMS AND WOMEN AFFAIRS:

Chastity and virginity are must traits for first times married brides, not so, however, for men.

Through Baggara history, probably, nothing has led to Baggara men death than fighting over women affairs – arguably women affairs lead to more death of Baggara than wars. Baggara men keep their women under close custody and watch them out from sex predators (virtually from any man). In many occasions, Baggara would kill a sexual predator right away in a spot in raging dogs' fight if they caught him; if he escapes and the damage was large, such as a woman gets pregnant or lost her virginity, the predator should be compelled to marry her. A dragging war between different Baggara clans may ensue if one clan sexually predating on another clan's women. Hundreds or more men might take up arms: spears, sticks, machetes, swards or even semi-automatic weapons with round of ammunitions and they take on the predating clan. In the past, a tribal Baggara war might inevitably ensued: many men could be killed, orphans would be left gazing at the blue, widows moaning and dusting their heads with ash, misery and complete chaos would be seen everywhere. A legendary *'Dahis wal-Ghabra'* Arabs' tribal wars story, which raged for forty years between the *Fazarah* and *'Ebs* Arab, may characterize the belligerent feudalism between Baggara clans over women affairs. Had the predator being a Baggara, his whole clan would have been taken by storm. In past times, a whole clan would be annihilated. Only when the perpetrator clan succumbs, then the war would subside and blood money paid for the deceased from both sides, and the predator would be compelled to marry his victim.

It is that belief held deep in the heart and mind of Baggara people that their dignity, honor and humility remain deeply entrenched in the chastity of their women. It is that belief of losing virginity, chastity and their dignity – their honorable virtuosity, lead them to an all-out war to restore the dignity of their clan, to bring peace to the ancestors and to be good in the eyes of competing clan. It is going to such extend that such wars named honor and dignity wars in past days.

Baggara families and tribes, who honorably fight over their women affairs, considered of the best class, and favored for marriages. Brides are much more scrutinized than grooms are during marriages on multitudes of traits - most of the traits, linked to chastity and its virtue – the virginity. Chastity of Baggara's women is not an easy trait; it is a complex social phenomena; chastity guarded by an unshakable Baggara's belief in the relationship between their dignity and chastity of their women. Messing around with their women would erode the dignity of their entire pedigree not only the immediate family. Century old dead holy fathers would be defamed had not had a harsh punishment would be precipitated upon sexual predators. It is outrageous for them to mess around with their women. The harshest punishment has to be served to restore peace, dignity and humility to families. It is their belief that the sex predator should have the harshest punishment, which leads them to a revenge fight, which may end up in a dead predator; it is such that punishment – death, the sex predators deserve to rid the Baggara families off the indignity and humiliation be fallen upon them.

A woman erodes her dignity and loses her social status, once and for all, once she jeopardizes her chastity.

Baggara has different attitudes regarding men chastity and virginity than that for women. A man of the messiest kind remains dignified as if he had not had done anything wrong. The rough fight with the sexual predator and hard beating of him over woman affairs is only to deter further messing with their women. The Baggara's man if he fornicated elsewhere and not caught, no one cares. He even could have told his fellow men what he was doing or what he would intent to do even with other Baggara's women, but not theirs. Taking this duality of Baggara behavior, from one side blaming women for sex outside wedlock and at the same time taking it easy with men, seems extremely odd and paradoxical. This conundrum is not only a Baggara behavior but also a deeply entrenched general Sudanese social behavior.

In Baggara social behavior, girlfriend, or boyfriend between boys and girls not allowed before marriage; even honest love not allowed before marriage; any love affairs totally forbidden and if discovered it will jeopardize the marriage of the couples; only on limited scale does Baggara start to open up to marrying women on the basis of love. The basic premise here is that, any relation between a woman and man that does not involve relatives considered a form of sexual infidelity. Boyfriend and girlfriend relationship are none-existent in Baggara land only under ultra-secretive cover. Nothing in Baggara culture called consensual sex. Any sex out of wedlock not only jeopardizes a woman's future marriage but also jeopardizes her females' siblings, and above all the status of their family as dignified family.

Honor killing is not prevalent for women, probably because of the fact that girls terrified to consider any relationship before their families choose their future husband. In addition, the way Baggara culture operates by honor killing male offender rather than targeting a woman, who involved in the act, helps alleviate honor killing of women.

In totality, Baggara social life and women affair deeply rooted in the Baggara culture and their way of life.

CIRCUMCISION:

Baggara zones considered land of circumcised people. Without any exception, nomadic Baggara men and women all circumcised. The circumcision phenomenon has strong religious and social implications among Baggara in particular, and Sudanese and Muslims people in general. For Muslims (most Sudanese are Muslims) practicing male circumcision is a religious call. An uncircumcised man cannot lead prayers and cannot slaughter any animal to be eaten by Muslims. It is socially and religiously unacceptable for a woman to marry or engage in sexual intercourse with an uncircumsized man.

Female circumcision is totally a different social phenomenon – it meant by Baggara, to be an essential part of properly raising a girl. Girls regarded as having been cleansed by the removal of their external female genital parts (Wikipedia, 2012). Circumcision ensures premarital virginity and inhibits extramarital sex. In her book "Emma's Wars", Deborah Scroggins eluted to the fact that, Baggara's women believe that Sudanese men enjoy sex with circumcised women. Such temptation lead to a phenomenon of re-circumcision of women each time they give birth – this is called *adal* (correction!). In Baggara culture, Baggara people practice one of the worst types of female circumcision - the so-called 'pharaonic circumcision', which practiced by Ancient Egypt under the Pharaohs (Wikipedia, 2012). They remove the clitoris, incise both labia, and tie the girl's legs together until the wound heals by joining the large labia together, and only leaving a small operture for urination. Tools used include razors, scalpels and sharp knives. Circumcision practiced without any use of anesthesia or detergent. Women practice circumcision for girls, while for boys circumcision mostly practiced on them by men. If the boy is young, a woman practitioner can circumcise him. In Baggara culture, circumcision usually practiced at young ages up to seven years old.

It is virtually useless to talk about uncircumcised Baggara men and women since all circumcised. It is one of the worst insults to say, "you are a son of uncircumcised" in the Baggara land – one has to brazen for a rough consequecies; it is equivalent to "son of a bitch" in the West.

Tea and Baggara Hospitality:

Baggara are extremely hospital people, and giving tea to their guests is symbolism of their best hospitality. If one is visiting Baggara people, he must have the habit of drinking tea; if not, Baggara will have an opinion about who he is. In their terms, one is a *Kamkali* person if he is not drinking tea (refers back to the text under "*Baramka* Social System" on the previous pages to see what meant to be a *Kamkali* person). For tea is a symbol of their hospitality. If one visits the Baggara and they do not have tea, Baggara stead fast to apologize that they do not have tea or sugar; in most cases, they apoloze before the guest notice the fact that they do not have tea. It is surprising to know that Baggara men, who are present when a guest visits them, they all order their wives to make tea for the gust, and all offer him tea. If the guest dares to reject the offer of tea from anyone of them, the host would be unhappy about the guest, since he feels the guest is not honoring him. It is an honor for them that one drinks from their tea even though he might just have more than one cup of tea from the others. Baggara have a rich tradition of making poems on tea and those who honor or dishonor tea drinking; the *Baramka* social system is the epic of the tea ceremonies and traditions.

Baggara hospitality extend beyond tea; they usually honor their guests by slaughtering animals in their honor; for a single person usually a Baggara man slaughter a rooster; for two or three guest they slaughter a lamb; for more than five they slaughter a male calf. During festivities, Baggara men show pride in the hospitality they extended to others; in many cases, a man might hang his prayer's bead around the neck of female praise singer (called *hakama*) and waits for a competitor, who will take off the bead to start counting how many animals each one slaughtered in honor of his guests. The winner of the competition cheered by the crowd and the competition event goes into their history notes – usually referring that year as the year when x person has beaten y person on hospitality contest.

Baggara hospitality can take different forms; in many times, they allow the guest to stay indefinitely if he wishes to stay. Always, when a guest comes he served with especial meals – not shared by everyone and they allow guests to sleep in their beds, matrices and use their blankets even if they do not have more ones.

Baggara go even further with their hospitality by sharing their wealth; if someone among Baggara lost his animal's wealth due thievery or accident, they collect animals per each Baggara person in the tribe or the immediate family (surra) to rebuild the lost herd. They offer one female calf if one names a child after one of them. They also offer milking cows for poor families to milk until their milk dry out and they bring them back for a replacement.

Baggara men freely share their food on a daily basis in a common place within the camp called *dara*. Everyone in the camp brings his dish and others are free to share. Guests are readily invited to eat as long as they stay in the camp. Hospitality deeply entrenched in the Baggara social system.

BAGGARA BRAVERY AND HUNTING OF ELEPHANTS:

Baggara legend has it that a *haday* - male praise singer, once upon a time, sang *heday* song praising one of a brave Baggara man named El Taib Baraka. He said *"El Taib of Baraka*, he is our son on the *farig* – the camp, but he is our brave hero when we go in a battlefield; burning charcoal well blown by strong wind resembles his sparkling red eyes; both of us – his people and his enemies stop short of where he stands in the battlefield". *Heday* is a type of lyrics that a singer (*haday*) sings in order to praise, or to disgrace someone. According to Baggara oral history, hero Taib never coward or he never gave in to any rivalry until his death. Baggara oral history overloaded with tales of heroes just as these of Red Indians chiefs in America. *Heday* lyrics such as Lonely Wolf lyrics sang on the honor of the Lonely Wolf chief of Red Indians are always sung for praise of Baggara *fursan* – heroes, using stringed instruments called *um kiki*. Women praise's singers called *hakamat* (sing. *hakama*) are instrumental part of Baggara war culture by igniting Baggara bravery during war times.

Baggara bravery well demonstrated during hunting of elephants in past days; usually a super *faris* - hero, such as hero Taib, has to lead the fight by approaching the elephant and engaging in a quick fight with it until the elephant gets agitated and then the *faris* runs toward where the rest of Baggara hunters are hiding. Once the *faris* passes with the elephant chasing him, the hunters come out from their hiding, and they pile on the elephant with their long-shafted spears. They target muscles of the elephant hind legs, on the upper part of the thigh, by using their large spears, which are characteristic of Baggara hunting spears. Once the elephant come down, the group immediately split into two different groups: one group continue to fight the elephant until they slaughter it, while the other group represents a protection force and takes defense positions around the slain elephant. Once the elephant falls, it will throw a loud voice as if weaning for help; it is of no doubt, and soon, a whole elephant's herd will come in rescue. The protection group will lead the fight with the elephants and tries to distract them in the same manner the *faris* enticed the elephant and led it to the group. It will be a long, dragging battle. Sometimes, the protection group wins by distracting the elephants away until the fallen elephant to be slaughtered. In other times, the elephants would defeat them, and in this case, they have to escape from the slain elephant; the elephants will stay for days around the fallen elephant until it heals and walks away with the herd or rots without allowing anyone to approach its corpse.

In Baggara culture, to bring down an elephant and to run away chased by elephants is very unacceptable. In this case, Baggara hunters labeled as cowards and *haday* and *hakamat* singers will take a heavy toll on them - morally.

Baggara bravery also appears in tribal or clans fighting and during raiding to own others' cattle in previous dark days of Baggara history.

BAGGARA CUPPING THERAPY (HIJAMA)

Hijama - literally sucking or suction, is the name in Arabs traditional medicine for cupping, where blood drawn by vacuum from a small skin incision for therapeutic purposes (Wikipedia, 2012). *Hijama* performed by Muslims as a form of alternative medicine, specifically mentioned and encouraged by the prophet Mohamed Teachings (*peace be upon him*). It mentioned in *hadith* – prophet teaching, "The *Hijama* is the best of your remedies" (*from Wikipedia article, cited: Hijama*). *Hijama* can be performed anywhere on the body, often at the site of an ache or pain in order to ease or alleviate it; it is most likely performed on the back on the sides of the spinal cord; it also often performed on the stomach, shoulders, sigh and the back of the neck.

Baggara practice two types of *hijama*, these are suction cupping and fire cupping. Old and middle-aged people practice the *hijama* more often than young people do; Baggara women practice fire cupping more than men do, while men practice suction cupping more often than women do.

Suction cupping is a unique form of dry cupping practiced by the Baggara; a procedure commonly involves creating a small area of low air pressure next to the skin by using a top part of an animal horn (known as *mahjam*) as suction tool. The procedure commonly used for relieving sour muscles or muscle ache or clotted blood. It involves two steps: placing the *mahjam* on the sour muscle or skin and sucking all air in the horn. The *mahjam* let for some time until the skin drawn up in a noticeable swelling. The tip of *mahjam*, always closed by a piece of bees' wax to prevent air from filling the vacuum created. The second step involves an incision of the swelled skin by a razor or any sharp tool – three incision made and the *mahjam* again applied to the same spot with strong suction as before and again the *mahjam* let for some times until the blood lets out into the *mahjam*. The blood removed from *mahjam* and it has to be cleaned before use. The procedure applied repeatedly to the same spot thereafter until no more blood drawn; at that point, it considered completed procedure. Sometimes, the *mahjam* used in dry cupping where skin drawn up as before by suction and the *mahjam* forcibly moved around the patient's body, where there is a pain, to help alleviate the pain or release the muscle contraction.

Fire cupping is a treatment where a piece of a newspaper (called *gurtas*) dipped in a little amount of fuel (sometimes the piece used without dipping into fuel) and lit, and the piece is then quickly inserted inside of the cup for a brief seconds. The cup then placed on the patient sour muscle. As small vacuum created by the combustion of the oxygen inside the cup, the skin drawn up into the cup creating a seal and the cup left until the drawn up skin grows many bubbles filled with yellowish body fluid (*the description adapted from Wikipedia article above to fit Baggara practicing of fire cupping*). Once the bubbles grow in size and number, the cup removed, and the bubbles purged to remove the body fluid. The alternative name for fire cupping is bubbling. Bubbling is noticeable method used by old women to remove backache and used for babies and toddlers to alleviate stomachache.

BAGGARA NEWBORNS CUSTOMS:

Newborns suckled first by a woman who already nursing a child. The woman will become the nonbiological mother for a child by suckling. This leads the child to be a son for the woman and all her daughters will be his sisters; he cannot marry anyone of them, although the woman may be a distant relative or not a relative at all. The suckling will guarantee that the child has a second mother or home if he loses his family.

Any newborn child cleanly shaved by the seventh day. At the same time he shaved, they slaughter a lamb (called *aghiga*) for celebrating his birth. The newborn also be awarded one female calf called (hair calf – *iglat al souf*). The single female calf becomes his wealth in the feature.

The newborn also will be circumcised as early as his seventh birth day. When separated from suckling, the child moves to his grandmother custody until he reaches age of becoming a cowboy then he moves to men place during daytime and sleeps with his peer boys during night times. The child has access to his mother all times; he can stay with his mother or even sleep with her in *drangal* – Baggara family bedstead.

Plate 1: A Baggara family – two of the kids are cousins to the family kids but they leave all their school terms with the family.

Plate 2: A Baggara man (his name sheikh Balal M Adam, with his family above, photographed by the author during August 2012 around El Hajiz city dressed in his traditional Baggara cowboys costume.

Plate 3: Two young Baggara girls colorfully dressed in their Baggara costume.

Plate 4: Young Baggara man wearing necklaces – bracelets, necklaces, rings and beads are usual accessories worn by young Baggara men.

Plate 5: Early morning Baggara gathering to drink morning tea. A photo taken on September 2012 during the rainy season.

Plate 6: Tea is their sole drink and it is the ensemble of Baggara hospitality. The man with the dark turban was a quest to others and enjoyed free tea.

Plate 7: Curiosity is one of well-known Baggara characteristics.

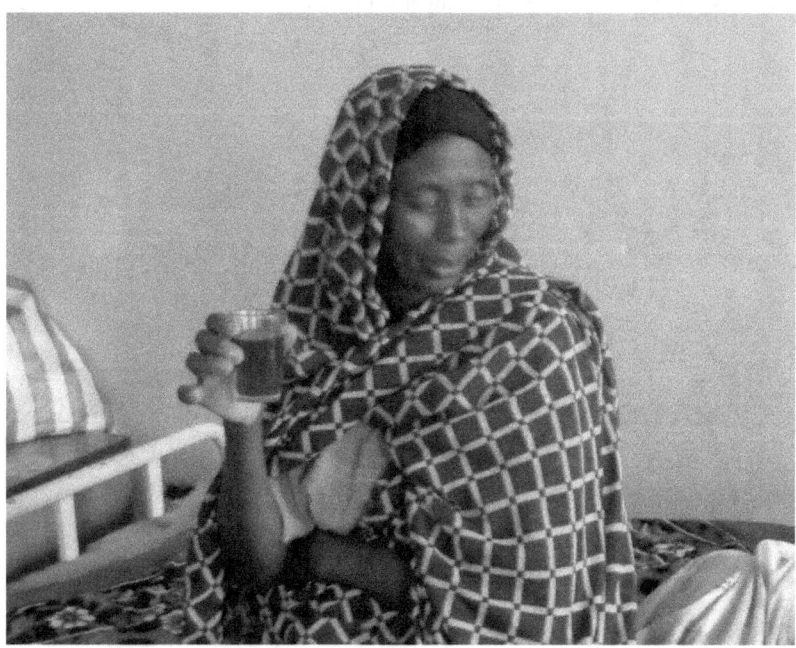

Plate 8: Characteristic way of holding a cup of tea by Baggara people; if one stick his finger at the bottom of the cup he will be charged by *Baramka* traditional court.

Plate 9: Lower lip sticking is characteristic of all Baggara women – a single facial scare also a dominant signal among most Baggara.

Plate 10: Curiosity is always there. Setting on fire using twigs and small branches is a daily routine to make morning tea.

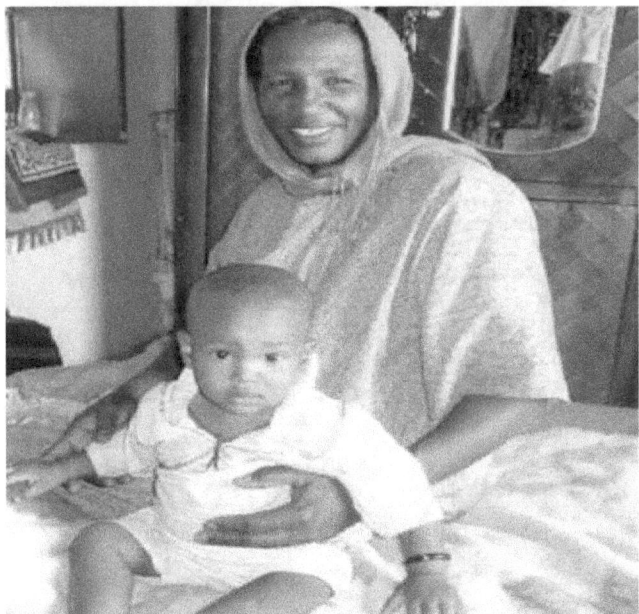

Plate 11: Baggara grandmothr cares for a grandson – one of a usual scene across Baggara tribes.

Plate 12: Baggara old men with their characteristic head caps (*taggia*) – Baggara old men are the voice of wisdom and reason in Baggara communities.

Plate 13: Young Baggara girls caring for their siblings – one of their main jobs in the Baggara family.

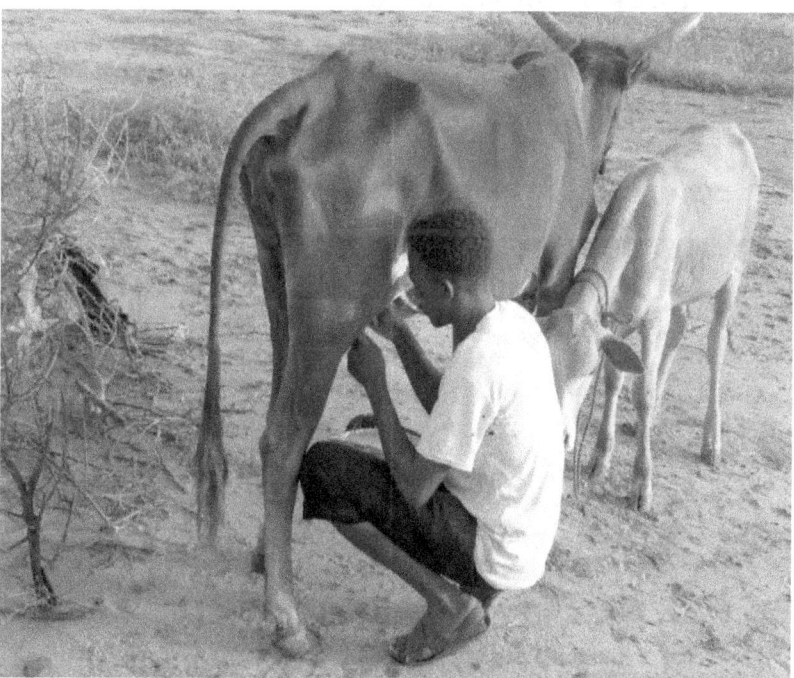

Plate 14: Milking cows in the Baggara way – calf is tied to the foreleg of the cow and milk bowl held tied between legs.

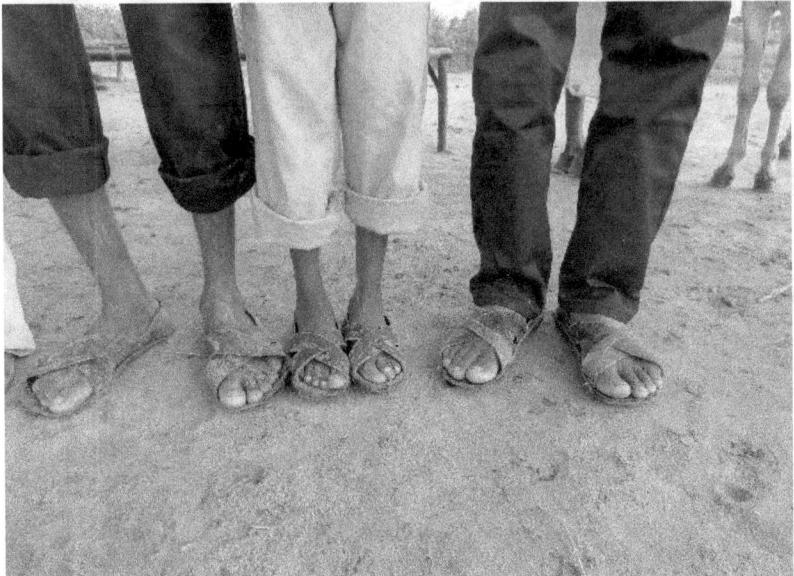

Plate 15: Baggara shoes made of tires - locally called (*tamout ta khali*, which means "the shoes will survive you").

Plate 16: Young Baggara man brushing his teeth using stick – Baggara use *Salvadora persica* (*arak*) tree and *Albizzia amara* (*arrad*) tree to brush.

Plate 17: Wearing a knife on left arm just lower or above biceps is characteristic for all Baggara men.

Plate 18: Young men lined up for a photo – showing their dress style.

Plate 19: Curiosity always there! – carrying stick with leather covering for hand is characteristic for some Baggara.

Plate 20: Baggara carry sticks and automatic guns and wear knife during usual day to day life.

Plate 21: Young Baggara men aiming with their AK-47s automatic weapons.

Plate 22: Baggara wrestling, well-known among Baggara Hawazma, Awlad Haymid and Missiriyya Zur in Kordofan region.

Plate 23: Baggara are cheerful people and always morale is upbeat during festivities.

Plate 24: Young Baggara woman showing off her luggage during a parade.

Plate 25: Baggara are colorful during dancing and festivities.

Plate 26: Norgara dance – all ages can participate.

Biraima M. Adam

5 SEASONALITY OF BAGGARA LIVELIHOOD

GENERAL BACKGROUND:

As in the case of early Greek civilizations, Baggara mostly view time as cyclic based on seasons of the year. It is enough to guess what Baggara livelihood looks like by only knowing the exact season of the year. Along the contours of seasons and environmental and ecological conditions, Baggara socioeconomic, social life, and livelihood follow repeatable seasonal patterns - season after season and year after year, Baggara follow a predicable lifestyle. The most clear and visible seasonality of their socioeconomic and livelihood occurs in two seasons: summer and rainy season.

BAGGARA LIVELIHOOD DURING SUMMER:

Summer is always a rough season for Baggara people.

Summer, in savannah region of Africa, is always gruesome season. In March, summer is in full swing and soon it reaches its peak early in May. It is a dazzlingly hot weather – temperature in a range of 40 °C (104 °F) is normal and can reach up to 45 °C (113 °F). During the summer season, Africa is as if set ablaze. Nature can curse every living being; it demands nothing less than complete surrender to its heat power. From dawn to dusk, the sun has absolute dominance over human activities, nature scenes, weather changes and undoubtedly a driving force for actions and interactions of organisms and matters. Yet the sun at savannah region has a majestically fascinating glory: when it rises in crystal-clear ball or when it fades away in azure and golden colors. Sound of early dawn prayers' reciting, birds' singing, Baggara herders hushing their animals to grazing ranges, and water-fetchers' utensils noise are just few ensembles of early dawn in savannah remoteness. Similarly, at dusk, sound of cattle or sheep chaotically mooing to their calves and kids, *nogara* drums trumpeted to bring in stray animals or to bring lost cowboys and shepherds home, are the essence of Baggara life in Sub-Saharan zone.

In a midsummer day, Baggara tend to limit their activities. The sun heat is a menace. The whole Africa continent turns into a vast glowing furnace - raging with heat and dust storms. Animals - such as goats, sheep and cows tightly pack under shade trees and are only able to graze either early morning or late evening. Lizards could run as fast as possible from their hiding places to climb nearby barely shaded trees. Creepers – such as chameleons, hedgehogs and turtles impatiently navigate their way as quickly as possible to nearby potholes. Crickets chirp loudly and feverishly from suffocating heat. Bees buzz continuously in their honey-wells to create a breeze for their queens and themselves. Nothing could sit on the rest except hibernating frogs, fish and reptiles; these animals bury themselves deep in clay soil before summer or encase themselves in cocoons to protect them from heat. Trees stand nakedly off their leaves; they had shed them off long time before summer toll and had taken their necessary protection – encasing themselves in thick wax layer to reduce their transpiration. Wind barely blows to create a breeze. Nothing could move around, they all stand still to lower their body temperature. Summer is an *eco-eclipse* in Africa.

Is it the hellish hell on earth! Surely, it is a nature curse! Sweat pours from human bodies from top to toes. The weather has extremely low humidity, while unusually high temperature. Yet, Baggara are well adapted to such Africa summer harshness; they use animals and insects sound to retreat to shade or to go about their normal life. When crickets chirp feverishly, Baggara order their kids to stay under shade trees. Baggara during summer, dig up wells to water their animals; also, they incline to eat less greasy foods and tend not to sell their animals at this time of the year, where animals are crumbling and weak.

Nothing resembles summer season in Africa in harshness; probably, except winter in northern North America, where trees shed off their leaves, bears enter in hibernation, Appalachian storms throw powdery snow dust or hurricane overwhelms regions with snowstorms: roads clotted in large snow piles and people cloaked in heavy winter clothing. As early dawn in Africa, sound of snow scrappers shoveling, roaring of salt-and-sand dispensers cleaning roads, whistling of wind on windows or echoing on mountains' tops are some ensembles of North America's winter weather calamities. Notwithstanding the differing feelings of heat in Africa or cold in North America, there is a common suffering of living organisms and common dimensions of human survival. It is not different for an Eskimo's child, who is shivering from freezing than a

Baggara's child, who is sweating from top to toes from scorching sun heat in Savannah region. Similarly, it is not differing for foxtail grasses in savannah region of African and those in America's Prairie brazing for a rough weather; and it is not that differ for hibernating frogs in savannah region of Africa during the summer and a hibernating bear in Antarctica during winter. All pushed by weather inclement to the limit of their physiological incapacities. Savannah region of sub-Saharan Africa remains a harsh, rough and unbearable hot in terms of weather conditions. Baggara, however, remarkably endured and prevailed in Africa.

During summer times, Baggara reach their most southern ranges; men engage in watering their animals, while women fetch water from far places in plastic jars carrying them a top their head for domestic home use. All work in daunting heat without any air-conditioning.

Apart from heat, summer in savannah of African has some picturesque silent beauty. Noticeable are changing landscapes and edaphic features. As winter in the West has its own sceneries, summer in Africa has its own unique sceneries, such as an ever-stretching span of flat terrains matted with dry and loosely strolling, termites-uprooted, yellowish grasses. Similarly, there are network of valleys covered with dense leaves-less skeletal vegetation. Clusters of mountains with varying stones' colors, shapes, and sizes appear far in sight as a background of panoramic view of rearing cows' herds. Knee-deep cracking clay in dry basins makes a reticulate of cracks as if an artwork; undulating creeks radiate from high mountainous land a waiting rainy season to carry water and silt to fertilize a sun-scorched low land, and the magnificent splendor of the sun rising and setting. All are beautiful sceneries noticed by Baggara people. Such summer landscapes require special taste for landscape to recognize their beautiful sceneries.

Lunar days are the best days in Baggara life during summer times.

Among the unique scenes of summer in Savannah region of Africa, is the lunar days. With clear sky and nothing to obstruct ones sight, the moon and stars appear crystal clear as the sun does. Constellations can easily be identified with the naked eye. Baggara youngsters gather during lunar days in open places during nighttime to chat or to dance – their singing, clapping and hard beating of ground with their feet could be heard from far a distance. Such night dance and chatting are well known as lunar days – locally called by Baggara as *layali el sammar*. Caravan travelers during lunar days enjoy their rides while being able to see almost as far as during daylight. Baggara grandmothers gather their grandsons to tell them axioms, puzzles, anecdotes, mythical stories, and linguistic art of mastering difficult and confusing tonque's twister words such as "*Sheikhi salakh sag sheikh el sheikh*" – which means: "my sheikh has slashed the leg of a sheikh who is a sheikh of someone called El Sheikh". Quickly repeating such tonque twisters words for many times can easily identify a dyslexic boy. Baggara's grandmothers are valued puzzlers; they use puzzles to sharpen their grandsons' mental capacities – such as asking a question: "something hitting a grass without making a noise, what is it?" the answer is – light. The grandmother goes on repeating the same question: "something hitting a grass without making a noise, what is it?" The answer is – shade; the grandmother can go on until the kids exhaust all possibilities; possible answers can be night, day, smoke, smell, sound, etc. In his excellent accounts of Baggara axioms and sayings, Mohyeldin Khail Elrayah (2003) said, "Baggara puzzles are oxymoron"- a figure of speech in which apparently contradictory terms appear in conjunction. In the example cited above, hitting should always produces a noise since it implies applying force, but Baggara puzzlers choose not.

During lunar days, Baggara women gather to work their hairs – to braid, de-braid or conglomerate their perfumes. Baggara's local perfumes made from crushed leaves, seeds, pots and wood from a range of aromatic plants - such as basil (*Ocimum basilicum*, Sudanese vernacular name; *rehan*) which is a common herb in Kordofan region of Sudan, mixed with animals' fats, oils and manufactured perfumes. During lunar days, Baggara people visit each other from distantly separated villages. A completely busy and active lunar nightlife springs up during lunar days. Importance and beauty of lunar days attributed in part to lack of urban centers and electricity in savannah region where Baggara live. Across savannah belt, there are few urban populated areas; the rest sparsely dwelled by villagers and Baggara nomads whenever a water source is available – as water represents the single most valuable life support in summer of savannah region. Lunar days represent a heavenly relief to savannah regions inhabitants - as they spend their day in daunting heat and hardwork to maintain their livelihood; they can gather as getaway.

Non-lunar summer nights in savannah region still have some benefits – almost all hunting during night times occurs during non-lunar days. As Baggara people in savannah lack electricity, light is of little value to them since they do not know its value or they rarely use it to beneficial use – apart from kindles at homes, light is only used in small cantons or village shops and even in case they use kerosenes. Baggara can walk long stretches of land during dark nights without any torches – though with their hands on their hearts not to step blindly on the most venomous Cobra sneaks. Darkness represents a get-away for unwelcomed activities, and it represents a shield to animals' thieves, who find cover from human eyes.

When summer approaches its end, Baggara at that time of the year, mostly they lack dairy products and they turn to eating less tasty food; their animals crumble due to lack of fodder and become of less economic worth. Baggara during this time become weak, skinny and sometimes boned. They sell less of their animals and tend to limit their expenditure, stop social life, reduce their buying power and turn to nature for survival. Summer has just hit the nerve of Baggara life. With trees shed off their leaves and time is over for fruit harvest or dairy products, Baggara turn to digging rhizomes, roots, underground stems and hunting of wild animals. At this time, crickets are feverishly chirping from heat; hibernating fish and frogs starting booing; morning birds artistically singing their early dawn songs. Without Baggara exact knowledge of what such phenomena mean, they, however, are sure of one thing that the rainy season is just few steps away to start.

BAGGARA LIVELIHOOD DURING *RUSHASH*:

After a long and dragging summer, signs of a new season called "*Rushash*" season (a pre-rainy-season) start to appear. A swirling hot air (and dust) springs up from nowhere, and keeps swirling for some distance and goes up high in the hot space vacuum. Baggara kids usually jump in the middle of the swirling dust and keep going. Old Baggara women and men think that it is satanic air; they recite some versus to fend it off. The swirling dust is a known phenomenon as hurricanes in the Americas, or tornadoes in the south East Asian islands. Because of high pressure and low air volume, an air vacuum created and quickly felled by cooler air. Variations in air pressure create the phenomenon of swirling dust. Baggara have their own explanation – it is satanic air.

Early in *Rushash*, a period of turbulence air currents continues for some time. Then soon the south-to-north wind starts blowing replacing the north-to-south one, which is persist summer long. Patchy clouds appear at afternoon in spare formations then clouds density gradually intensifies day after day to build voluminous mountains of clouds in the sky. Trees break into noticeable green shoots of buds. Temperature drops during day time, though, it is exceptionally warm weather during night time - a high conviction heat bother everyone along savannah region; during this time, Baggara people sleep outside their domes in the yards. Although it is a short period, not more than one and half months, however, this short season is distinct from the summer and the following rainy season. It has it is own ecological and human dimensions that might warrant a separate name for such a season – Baggara called it breezy season (in Arabic terms *Rushash*).

Rushash season has distinct characteristics – it is characterized by a sweet, refreshing blow of air breeze called *duash*. When it breezes, Baggara's herds lift their heads up and nose toward where the breeze blows. Every time such the breeze blows, one could hear a sigh of relief and murmuring that the rainy season is close. Migratory birds fly during *Rushash* in large flocks; monkeys packs cross areas in a large number; and flocks of guinea fowls cackle day long. Along savannah region, farmers at this time of the year start cleaning their farms from crop remains of the previous season, burning stumps, uprooting trees to open new fields, buying or making new farming tools, repairing their huts, and collecting firewood and storing it for use in the rainy season. Villagers gear their effort for a new rough season of farming, mosquitoes bites, tsetse flies, mud, mosquitoes' nets, sleeping early and waking up early, eating less tasty food and sometimes hunger. Baggara nomads, however, yearn for a new, hopeful season: the herding season where rains become steady and ready to migrate to their northern grazing ranges. Along such lines of human-ecological association, farmers are now moving toward a distressing, hard and laborious season – the farming season, while Baggara nomads aiming for their best season throughout their grazing year – the herding season.

BAGGARA LIVELIHOOD DURING HERDING SEASON:

Rainy season turns savannah region in a wilderness of greenery and lush vegetation.

During rainy seasons in savannah region of Africa, rains could rain during a whole day or afternoon or night times; echoing thunder and lightings are usual rainy season *chores*. When it rains it pours, flash flood may sweep large plains. Baggara nomads quickly hush their animals and move miles away upland to their rainy season grazing areas - where vegetation and grasses are short. High savannah quickly becomes a jungle after rains start. Valleys, carry muddy water, may stop movement altogether to or from cities to villages. High savannah grasses grow on cut-and-fill roads; branches close the spaces between trees and climbing vegetation form a thick reticulate networks impeding movement. Mosquitoes, harmful flies and bugs breed in record numbers, and they can bother humans on broad daylight. High savannah no longer could be suitable for human habitation. Farmers, in high savannah, enter one of the roughest times in their year: they work day long uprooting grasses with their bared hands, eat little of nutritious food, sleep less due to flies and mosquitoes, walk knee-deep in mud, people drop their human remains near to their homes or on roads and they drop any other activities other than farming. Villages turn into filthy trash of human waste; smoke emits from every hut to fend of harmful flies, and there is nothing of any leisure time or even nowhere to go other than farms. About two and half months have to pass before farmers can see any light of hope of a new harvesting season starts to appear – if rains are abundant, then youngsters start to dance during lunar days. Yet farmers in high savannah region have their own way of alleviating the stress; they go in group farming - locally called *naffir* – chanting, singing, women cooking and men cleaning one of their member farmer's farm. Such activity rotates among farmers on a weekly basis until the farming season is over – creating their own microcosm of seasonal activities.

Usually, Baggara who lose their animals settle in villages and become part of village norms. They, however, resent the village life and yearn to go back to the nomadic life, but rarely they make it back to nomadism instead they continue to live their whole life on pleasant memories of their past nomadic life.

Low savannah region inhabitants are far less distressed than high savannah region dwellers during the rainy season. In low savannah region, vegetation are short, trees are less closed, environmental conditions are favorable – sandy dunes with less mud and less harmful flies, bustling common marketplaces are open, buying and selling of animals and goods are steady, aromatic plants scent environment with fresh autumn breeze. However still a sense of farming season persists – farmers go to their farms on a daily basis to tend them or protect them from animals since nomads move north to low savannah region.

Once rains become steady, Baggara nomads move far north to lowland vegetation areas, such as Northern Kordofan region of Sudan. There, in low savannah, nomads engage in selling milk products in local markets, selling their animals to traders, buy new cloth and dome utensils, and a sense of relief encompass nomads ranges. Youth engages in wrestling matches, dance and marriage celebrations. By the time Baggara nomads reach their rainy grazing season, trees already blossom in colorful flowers, aromatic plants and basils (*Ocimum Basilicum* L, locally called *rihan*) and toothbrush tree (*Salvadora persica*, local name *arak*) infuse the environment with a pleasant autumn scent. Lilies (*Nymphaea spp*, local name: *sitaib*) grow beautiful white flowers and lush green leaves in water pools, and sandpipers and other wading birds waddle with their checks alongside sandy watercourses. Baggara nomads enjoy their herding season and livelihood: horns sound be heard from miles away alerting to the presence of a superstar wrestler, *nogara* drum dancing is usual scene, wrestling matches organized across the spectrum of Baggara nomad's camps and, cowboys enjoy decorating their bulls for bull fight. A new relaxing and engaging spirit flourishes on all Baggara camps. Yet, looking back to their kin Baggara farmers in high savannah zones, they still muddied deeply in their hardships – and their hardships aggravate as the rainy season progresses until harvesting season. For Baggara people, hardships and suffering of villages during the rainy season make them feel proud of their nomadic movement and give them an air of superiority of way of their life.

Rainy season turns low savannah in one of the most beautiful and picturesque scenery in Africa.

Baggara have beautiful poems and sayings praising their way of life and rainy season such as: "Which is better: is it a sound of a young calf among flowering acacia trees or sound of donkey inside a village quarter". For Baggara, it is no brainer that flowering plants are beautiful than a village quarter, and so it does a sound of a calf among the flowering plant than a donkey sound in the village – Baggara are passionate cattle herders. During the rainy season, Baggara go about their daily life with an air of pride. The gentle men always dress in their Arabian princes' lofty costumes, others in their gladiator's dress. Women carry varieties of silver and golden rings, nostrils, necklaces, sliver crowns and beautiful clothing and accessories. They enjoy admiring themselves with dense masker makeup, lips dying, hair braiding and styling - with a mixed cream of perfumes, herbs, sandalwood and others. The youth become more enthusiastic about festivities, dancing and socializing. During this time of the year, Baggara do nothing but rhetorical carnivals and festivities. Like Latin Americans during world models or Mexican carnivals, Baggara stay upbeat and fully immersed in festivities: dancing and wrestling.

Baggara life cannot be any better than during the rainy season. It is an ultimate happiness fueled by relief from tumultuous summer and dragging movement to their rainy season grazing land. With such outpouring emotional ceremonies, Baggara, in essence, are relieving themselves from spillover of rough times and peeking ahead to another long dry summer or may just enjoying the occasion. Baggara's life is a life inseparable from the ecosystem in which it exists. Whether heaven throws to them rains or dust, their life shaped and fashioned accordingly. In the Baggara land, climate has the ultimate command in every sense of their life: their marriage, wedding, festivals, rituals, schooling, including their own existence.

BAGGARA LIVELIHOOD DURING WINTER SEASON:

When winter season begins, trees shed of their leaves, grasses wilt, seasonal water pools become muddy and eventually dry out, crops ripe for harvest; and nomads are ready to move gradually back across low savannah zone to high savannah areas, where there they pass their summer time. Winter across savannah region is the harvest season – people harvest their crops, enjoy seasonal festivities, fresh crops, cheap prices and most of all high savannah opens up, where people can visit cities and marketplaces. A new rebirth of life injected into the body of savannah land. Villagers start their usual harvest dance and rituals. Fresh maize and groundnuts are barbequed on open places. Villagers and nomads burn tall savannah grasses early in winter season. Buring leads to opening up of spaces around villages and allowing for new growth of new shoots. The new re-growth of grasses called *harig* grasses, which are succulent grasses.

During winter movement to their summer grazing areas, Baggara endure daunting activities: they have to move their animals for long distance to find water-places; they endure cold and dry winter weather; they have to break up tall grasses and open up seasonal migration routes and they have to survive lot of issues related to cattle breaking into farmers' crops.

Winter in savannah region is another unique season. Nature scenes dominated by yellowish leaves, sand dust, and windy, cold weather.

Seasonality of environmental and ecological conditions has led to seasonality of Baggara life and activities – marriages, festivities, harvesting rituals, schooling, herding, and even hunting are seasonal activities.

Plate 27: Panoramic view of Baggara herds during the rainy season.

Plate 28: Baggara Zebu cows (*Bos primigenius indicus* or *Bos indicus*)

. Plate 29: Early in the rainy season (called Rushash) scene of Baggara cows grazing on the new growth of grasses.

Plate 30: Early morning scene in a Baggara camp during the rainy season.

6 BAGGARA CULTURE: ETHNIC KNOWLEDGE OF ENVIRONMENT

As nomads, Baggara are greatly in need of knowledge to predict events and processes occurring in the environment in which they live. It is fascinating for someone to know that with the large volume of common humankind knowledge to predict weather conditions, environmental and ecological changes, Baggara use their own cultural and ethnic knowledge to cope with their environment.

Baggara possess unique forms of cultural and ethnic knowledge, that they effectively use to predict when rains start or end. In additions, there are myriad of things or processes that they try to know or understand based on such cultural knowledge. Baggara as nomads have developed different cognitive means to deal with environment conditions and changes. They, always, find that they are, in need to know: when does rainy season start? When does it stop? Where abundant underground water exists? How does underground water located? How desirable grazing recognized? When insects and harmful flies to their animals outbreak? When they can move out of high savannah before mud becoming an impediment factor to their movement?

Looking into such questions reveals four common factors that affect Baggara seasonal migration and their livelihood; these are rains, vegetation, insects and mud. Cunnison (1966) already explored in considerable depth how these factors affect the transhumance life of Missiriyya Humr – one of Baggara tribes.

These four factors - rains, vegetation, insects and mud, are the most important in the lives of savannah nomads. Baggara not only know about these factors, but also they try to predict their likely effects on their movements. Baggara ethnic knowledge to deal with these factors is mostly ecological in nature. When the Baggara see certain phenomenon, such as a blossom of certain vegetation, which happens to be just before rains start or when certain vegetation shed their leaves before rains begin, the Baggara use such blossom or, lack of it, as an indicator of the nearing or ending of rains. There are four underlining elements that are keys in the Baggara knowledge about the factors that shape their seasonal migration and livelihood, these are: animals (sounds, nesting periods, migrations, etc.), insects (sounds, chirping, outbreaks etc.), vegetation phenology (budding, blossom, flowering, fruits ripening, leaves shedding etc.), celestial objects movement (movements or orientations of stars, galaxies, constellations etc.). Following are some description of how Baggara use these elements as predicates for environmental events, such as start or end of rains, in order for them to move in their transhumance movement to be in the right place and at the right time:

ANIMALS BEHAVIORS:

Baggara use many types of animals' behaviors as predicates for environmental events, among such animals are birds, reptiles, fish, and even large games. One of such animals is a lungfish (locally called *um korou* fish). When rains stop, this fish buries itself deep in clay soil and enters a hibernating mode, however according to Baggara oral stories, this fish is not hibernating, but continues to eat from its tail fins. As summer progresses and gets prolonged, the fish consumes its fins and starts cannibalizing on its tail. At this point, the lungfish starts an annoying noise such as boua boua boua. Once the Baggara hear the fish's annoying sound, they gear up for longer summer period; they say the summer is dragging, and they start to cope with its likely adverse effect. Possibly, they order more animals' rations or sharpen their axes to cut trees to feed their animals. Baggara never eat this fish, and they hate to catch it. When Baggara boys catch it, they immediately throw it back into the water and run away shivering from fear.

Some questions spring up to mind about Baggara attitudes toward this lungfish: why do they not eat it? Why they hate it? Why they assume that when this fish starts its annoying sound that the summer is dragging? Clearly, it is a psychological matter for Baggara not to eat this fish, since it eats itself, even though the meat it eats is fish meat – for it is a cannibal animal! Cannibalism is abhorrent for anyone. Why Baggara assume the summer is dragging? Is it possible that the fish will be crying from pain of eating itself? Does the fish might be crying from heat or hunger? Is it possible the fish is happy about the nearing of rains to stop the pain of eating itself? No one knows. However, nothing can justify to the Baggara otherwise except the fact that the summer prolonged, and they have to do whatever necessary to feed their animals. If Baggara see someone lazing around without being up to challenges of the assumed prolonged summer, they tout him "eeek man, why lazing around, the *um korou* fish cried and you have not yet sharpened your axe to cut trees to feed your herd!" Let us turn and closely look to the fact of that annoying fish sound as a predictor or predicates of a dragging summer! Does it sound strange? Is there any truth that the lungfish knows that the summer is dragging? How (in the world!) does such hibernating lungfish know about weather conditions? Absolutely nothing will dissuade Baggara from believing that the summer is dragging. For Baggara, it is like weather prediction news; they digest it, burn it in and do whatever necessary.

Birds used similarly to lungfish as environmental predicates. One such bird is singing black sparrowhawk (the author faced some degrees of uncertainty of misidentifying this bird, but to the best of the author knowledge it is a black sparrowhawk; locally this bird called *mi'atieb*,). Ali H. Saleh (2004 p. 257) mentioned the name of this bird as used by Hawazma as mi'ateib (written in Arabic: معيطيب). These black sparrowhawks are enemies to crows and scavenger birds. Whenever they find crows or eagles start a fight, and they strike them with full force chasing them up on the sky twisting and curving around in a similar fashion to space warfare or fight them through trees branches. Sometimes, crows get exhausted from flying and, eventually, land on the ground walking, but still the bird keeps on an intensifying aggressive fighting. These types of sparrows have sharp clowns and peeks. Baggara never eat this bird, yet they love to hear it is singing and it is unbelievably sweet chirping tempo early on the morning when summer approaching its end. A refreshing mood spreads on the Baggara camps saying summer approaching an end. Why Baggara do not eat this sparrow? Is it because of its sweet chirping? Is it because it is a brave bird and since Baggara honor bravery, they do love it for that reason? Does it look like scavenger rather than a bird? On the other hand, does it because it chirps early in order to wake them up, to take their animals to grazing or watering or, waking them up for dawn prayer. Do such reasons have any effect on their decision not to eat it? Whatever reasons or justifications maybe, the underlying fact is that Baggara do not eat this bird. However, most importantly how Baggara know that when these sparrows chirp early in the morning that the summer approaching an end? Do sparrowhawks have any knowledge about the weather conditions? Alternatively, why sparrowhawks chirp early on the morning when summer approaches an end? Obviously, Baggara do not care to answer such questions. However, whatever reasons the sparrowhawks chirp - whether because it is a fertilization period or, because there is too much convection heat bothering them during this time of the season or, because the bird is happy about weather changes, Baggara know only one thing: the summer end is approaching and they have to prepare themselves for the rainy season. At such time, Baggara, most likely, start preparing ropes, saddles and mats for their seasonal rainy season journey.

Baggara use migratory birds decidedly as indicators of seasons beginning or ending. Such birds may include cattle egrets, ducks, guinea fowls, black and white storks, toucans and many more.

Black storks (called *simbria* or simply *simbr*) are among notable birds, when they appear on trees tops it means to Baggara rainy season is steady. Baggara kids usually sing songs when they see black storks: "oh storks with long peek, when your father's grains grow. Oh they grow when soldiers come". This clearly indicates that to Baggara should start to sow their grains, which indicates a planting season when black storks appear. Similarly, Baggara use white storks (called *abu ghanam* or *abun ghanam*, the word *ghanam* means sheep, for them these birds look like white sheep with black nose) as an indicator of the harvesting season when they appear. Usually, white storks appear in a large number on high savannah areas when seasonal grass fires break out and fry locusts and grasshoppers. When toucan birds (*Tockus erythrorhynchus*, called locally *abu mangoor*, means large billed bird) start to migrate north, it is a right time for Baggara to start their seasonal movement toward their rainy herding season. When toucans migrate southward after their captive females (usually the male toucan puts his female on wood cracks during nesting and closes the crack with mud) get out of their nest together with their new chicks, then it is time for Baggara to move toward their summer season location. Baggara do not eat birds such as storks or cranes or, neither their eggs. The question is why do not they eat them? Is it because such birds are beautiful? Do they smell when cooked? What is about their eggs? Baggara do not eat many birds, which migrate through their grazing ranges. How Baggara come to know that such birds are indicators to seasons start or end when they come migrating through their rangelands? One may know the answer, however, whatever reasons that these birds migrate, Baggara know only that these birds come about their places because the rainy season is either starting or started or it is ending.

Baggara, as they use birds to know when the rainy season starts or stops, they also use birds for good fortune or bad luck. Among birds used for good luck are small white falcons, cattle egrets (called *abou rahou*) and hoopoes (Sudanese vernacular name *hoodhud*, Baggara call it *abun tagag* – kicker bird). Baggara also claim good fortune if they see crown cranes dancing. Crown cranes are one of the most elegant and beautiful bird's species in swampy marshes of high savannah region of Africa. Ground-hornbill bird (locally called *abun duluk*) used as an indicator of bad luck. This large-sized African bird characterized by black coloration and vivid red-colored face and throat patches (yellow in juvenile birds). The white tips of the wings (primary feathers) seen in flight are another indicative characteristic. Whenever Baggara see ground-hornbill, they say "give us your white wings' tips and take to the rest of your black feathers), such sayings believed to relief the bad luck. One of very bad luck occasion for Baggara is to find an egg of Savannah Nightjar (*Caprimulgus affinis*, locally called: *um kititi* bird), or pennant-winged nightjar (*Macrodipteryx vexillarius*, locally called either *um kititi* or *um al ri'yan*). Finding an egg of these birds is just like a nightmare for Baggara – it believed across Baggara tribes that the eggs of these birds bring bad luck, specifically a death of one parent. Who is going to die – a mother or father? It depends on the action one takes upon finding the nightmare eggs. If one chooses to take the egg, Baggara say it will kill the mother, but if one chooses to leave the egg, they say it will kill the father. Whenever Baggara find the egg, they face with a dilemma that, who they decide to kill from their parents. To the Baggara very best luck, the eggs of these birds are hard to find due to their camouflaged color. It is a rare occasion to find one, but if one does then he will face the hard decision.

Gazelles, although, they are elegant and beautiful animals, but when they cross through Baggara camp or village, usually Baggara consider this as bad luck where they assume the village eventually will be abandoned.

Baggara also use reptiles such as large lizards. Among the best-known reptiles are the savannah dragons or *monitors* (called locally *waral*). Usually, when Baggara hear savannah dragons bark like a dog during night times it is for sure to them the rainy season approaching an end. savannah dragons are usually silent animals, or they do hissing sound, but only occasionally they bark loud and to the Baggara it is only happening when the rainy season approaches its end. How in the world Baggara know that this creature is barking because the rainy season is ending? What if this creature is happy about ending of rainy season? Alternatively, what if it is barking because of it is a breeding season? Again, whatever reasons maybe, Baggara know only the savannah dragon barked because of the rainy season is over. Accordingly, Baggara start to prepare water-carrying utensils such as *girab* (water carriers made from animal leather) or buy plastic water jars. They spread the word out that *waral* barked, and this is enough to indicate what should be done for this time of the season: they should be ready for a long movement to their summer location and it is most importantly there are no more rains when the dragons bark, the rainy season almost ended. One can contemplate if the savannah dragon barked in India, does that mean the same thing as do Baggara in sub-Saharan Africa think it is the rainy season ending.

Culturally, Baggara, somehow, strongly believe the instinct of animals to sense environmental events. It well known to Baggara that animals such as dogs and cats can sense the volcanoes before they erupt, and in a similar fashion, they use most of the animals in their local areas to sense a change in the environment in which they live.

INSECTS OUTBREAK:

Phrases such as "Insects have chased us" or "We are attacked by flies" or "Insects biting us" are common among Baggara when they are not yet out of high savannah region during rainy season. Baggara are helpless and defenseless when it comes to dealing with insects; their best bet is to flee and abandon the area until the end of the rainy season. Baggara have to stay away until the insects complete their lifecycle before they can sneak back into the region. Anecdotally, Baggara say if one's child held hostage one can fight back to release him, but, with the outbreak of harmful insects, one have no chance even to look for him, one have to run away - conditionally. Baggara's cattle exhibit similar behavior; it is usual to see cattle run from the range to quarters or mass together to defend each other against the insects attack; it is one of the rare instances when a cow abandons her young born calf and run away to safety. Running away or fleeing could be well argued that it is one of the best cultural adaption of Baggara to deal with such dire situations.

In contrast to Baggara nomads, settlers of high savannah region cope with the situation by sleeping early in nets and smoking their huts with every unwelcoming repellent, such as animal's dung and green branches, which emit pungent smell, to repel the insects. They limit their social activities during night times, stop moving around late and limit their motion during sleeping. Some indigenous population of high savannah dwells on mountains tops at high altitude to stay above the level of the flies' prevalence.

Insects, in Africa, are diverse and numerous, especially in high savannah region. Among some of the most notorious insects in savannah region that affect Baggara life, are tsetse flies, horseflies, mosquitoes, aphids (locally known as *njifat*), ticks and spiders. Although Baggara use such insects as indicators of how environment is unsuitable for them. They, also, use other types of harmless insects, which live in colonies and outbreak in record numbers in response to rains, such as termites and ants, as environmental change predicates.

Tsetse flies cause sleep sickness and tsetse fly disease for Baggara and their animals. However, tsetse flies are now rare due to severe change in climate. Horsefly is common across Baggara rangeland. Baggara know what environmental and ecological conditions are suitable for the outbreak of both of these insects: when trees grow dense canopies, rainfall intensifies and grasses grow, especially, when trees species such as *Combretum* species (locally called: *habil*, see vegetation sub section below) develop closed canopy early in the rainy season. Once the tsetse flies or horseflies break, Baggara immediately move north, or they move from closed forest areas into open spaces. Early during the rainy season, Baggara make smoke fires, during evening time, using green branches, twigs, and climbers to smoke the fly. The tsetse flies and horseflies are especially active during evening times, although, the flies keep active during most of midday and afternoon. As the rainy season progresses, the flies become intolerable to both Baggara and their animals alike. It is a must for them to get out of the high savannah regions and start their transhumance movement to the northern zones of their ranges where vegetation are sparse and, no harmful tsetse flies, though horseflies may still exist but in a tolerable numbers. It is only because of these flies that Baggara leave the high savannah, in most cases, and rush away leaving many unfinished businesses behind, such as farming. The flies have severe socioeconomic effects - apart from the notorious sicknesses – they cause Baggara to get their school kids off schools prematurely before the end of school terms, which lead to large school dropout. Baggara have no means to deal with the tsetse flies or horseflies except to run away or wait for the fate of their animal; if the animal caught the disease – either, it will die or get well without any treatment from them; the only thing Baggara can do is to smoke the flies and mosquitoes from the victim animal. One of the known plants that used by Baggara is veldt grape (*Cissus quadran gularis,* called locally *salala'a*). Baggara, traditionally, use veldt grape as insects repellent – a usage that is seems to be unique to Baggara people. It is known elsewhere that the plant used in traditional medicine as anti-inflammatory, for treating obesity, diabetes, heart diseases, high cholesterol and healing fractured bones. The plant also used traditionally to support optimal joint health, enhance recovery, support healthy weight management and, as an antioxidant. Baggara people consider none of such usages. Baggara cut down the succulent stems, and pile them on large burning fires; a dense, pungent smoke is released, which repels the insects and, it is a potent repellent for any insect.

Mosquitoes well known to cause Malaria disease, but, mostly, it is unknown to Baggara what mosquitoes can cause to their animals except a disease which causes their cattle to become weak, lose appetite and crumble. Animals cannot cope with mosquitoes; they will keep moving around nightlong and settle to rest only during the early morning hours. Baggara use animals' dungs smoke to fend away mosquitoes, from animals and themselves. Baggara rarely used to using mosquitoes nets; they usually brave the fly and when they get the Malaria disease, they deal with it through local medicinal herbs and plants. Mosquitoes cause similar socioeconomic factors as tsetse flies and significantly contribute to transhumance life mode of Baggara through high- and low-savannah regions.

One of the mosquitoes types locally called *"gheem"*, an exceedingly tiny insect which outbreaks early during evening time and then disappears or dies during daytime, is one of the most annoying and unbearable menace to Baggara and their animals. In 1844, Pallme wrote in his book: Travels in Kordofan, talking about Baggara, said that: "But their greatest plague is a little animal, called Johara, - a fly which makes its appearance in large numbers, in many regions, in central Africa, in the rainy season and proves terribly destructive. Its bite is harmless to man, but the more dangerous to cattle and instances are on the record, in several regions, of whole herds having been destroyed by the vermin in a remarkably short time". Pallme continued to say "This insect is also the chief cause of the Baggara leaving these parts of the country, which are otherwise so safe for them, and so advantageous for their cattle; it forces them, in fact, to deliver themselves into the hands of the Turks". The Turks were occupying Sudan at that time, and they known for their cruelty and plundering of Baggara nomads to extract taxation of their animals and use their oxen for travelling army ammunitions. Insects proved so powerful to chase Baggara right into their enemy territories.

Almost 500 years later of their existence in high savannah region of Africa, Baggara still keep running away from insects during the rainy season, year after year.

VEGETATION PHENOLOGY:

Vegetation Phenology is the study of periodic plant life cycle events and how these influenced by seasonal and interannual variations in climate (Wikipeda, Phenology, 2012). Baggara use the term growth instead of phenology to describe variations in phenology (*el nabat gam* means plants grown; *al gash gam* means grasses grown; *al gash nawar* means grasses grown flower; *al gash nigid* means grasses matured, *al gash hata al iyyal* means grasses dispersed seeds. Replacing the word *al gash* with *al nabat* leads to plants stages).

Among the best known vegetation to predict rainy season across Sudanese cultural contours is *Acacia albida* tree (called locally *haraz*). The phrase "*Haraz* war against rains" known to all Sudanese as *haraz* trees dislike rains, and for that reason shed off their leaves when rainy season approaching. Such Sudanese cultural attitude toward *haraz* phenomenon is just cress-crossing with Baggara mentality about vegetation phenology as predicates of rainy season. Baggara use a large array of plants to predict or monitor rains and rainy season. Reflecting for a moment about "*Haraz* war against rains" phrase: Does *Acacia albida* knows that rain is approaching and purposely shed off its leaves? Why it sheds off its leaves from rains? Alternatively, how Baggara know it is shedding off leaves because it dislikes rains? It turns out that *Acacia albida* is an introduced species from Indian subcontinent, and it happens that its leaves shedding season, there, is equating to the beginning of rainy season in Sudan. In essence, *Acacia albida* trees kept their biological clock unaltered, which seem odd for introduced tree species, which mostly adapt to the new environment or may fail. It turns, Baggara care only about whether the *haraz* trees predicating rainy season or not! It is true in this sense, that the tree is excellent predicator of the start of the rainy season or most likely summer ending.

Baggara use many trees to predict the event of the rainy season. Trees such as *Albizia* species (locally called: *arrad*) trees and *Combretum* species (locally called: *habil*) trees used to predict when rains start. *Habil* trees grow lush green and dense leaves before rains start. For Baggara, it is usually taking about two months from *habil* budding to starting of rains. It is well known in areas of savannah as South Kordofan of Sudan that when *habil* branches close, it is about time for rains to start. Baggara are aware of trees phenology (bud growth, leaving, flowering, fruit growth etc.) in relation to environmental conditions. Usually, trees buds in new shoots in relation to certain precursors in the environment. Such a phenomenon is much clear in the Northern hemisphere when Oaks, Platanus or Myrtle trees break new buds during spring time; it is much less clear in savannah region of Africa where temperature regime changes are not that drastic between summer and the start of the rainy season. However, Baggara are keen about their knowledge that, *habil* trees new shoots means nothing to them unless grown in full, dense vegetation cover, at that point they say rain is coming soon. It is tempting to think that *habil* trees always grow green shoots at the same time of the year; this is not the case in almost every tree species. Trees affected by environmental, ecological and edaphic conditions in similar ways animals affected by food nutrition. *Habil* trees may start budding early in April, but due to some environmental conditions may not grow in full canopy only after three months; alternatively, it may grow to a closed canopy within two months if conditions are favorable. It is unimportant to Baggara to know what environmental conditions that affect the *habil* growth, but it is only matter to them that a full canopy develop before it is time for rains start.

Albizia species (*arrad*) are among trees species that Baggara use to predict rainy season in a similar fashion to using *habil*, but here Baggara only consider new shoot growth. If the new shoot of *arrad* tree grows to about an armlength long, then, Baggara considers that as a sign of the rainy season. Baggara also use *arrad* in some spiritual sense; when Baggara move in places of cracking clay, usually they do not like rains to fall, since rains in this case create an impeding muddy situation. In such case, Baggara religious sheikhs or any religious person asked to recites some Qur'anic verses to fend of rains and mostly they use a branch from *arrad* tree. The religious sheikh will recite and occasionally spits on the branch and points to the clouds to direct them where to move or to rain. After doing the recitation on the branch, the sheikh orders the youth to carry the branch and, they stick it upright on a crack near a top of the tree. The sheikh and youth will patiently a wait and observing the branch, hopping that the wind will not blow it off the tree. If the branch blows off by the wind, then the group rushes toward their quarters, to shelter themselves from rain. Questioning Baggara wisdom, why only *arrad* tree has this spiritual sense to them? How they come about this idea of reciting on the branch to fend off the rain? It is known in holly hadith said by prophet Mohamed (peace be upon him) used to say for rains: "around us, but, not on us". Baggara build their own cultural practice to fending off rains using *arrad* branches or even other trees branches if no *arrad* tree is available, yet *Albizia* species might not even present in Arabia to support their religious practices! Such practices may come from sophism sects to which Baggara are arduous followers.

As Baggara use vegetation to predict when rains start or stop, they also use vegetation to predict underground water availability and even the nutritional value of grazing. Baggara use *Bauhinia rufescens* (locally called: *kharoub*) and *Crateva adansonii* (locally called: *debkar*) to locate places for underground water. *Debkar* trees, usually, grow along seasonal streams beds; similarly, *Kharoub* grows on seasonal *wadis* and water pools. These trees are deciduous in dry, and semiarid areas, however, they turn into evergreen in high rainfall areas or when there is abundant underground water.

As animals' rangers, Baggara know which trees or grasses are desirable to their animals, but the remarkable criterion about this cultural knowledge is how it passes from generation to generation without written documentations and usually passes to young cowboys at unusually early age. Ahmed S. El Wakeel, et. al (1993) identified fourteen herbaceous species in Table 4 as desirable species. Baggara nomads knew these species historically, and it is a common knowledge to them; the vernacular names used in Table 4 are common Baggara names for these grasses; they use these names across Baggara communities or tribal lineage. Baggara always look for these species to graze their animals. They even know which one will yield greater milk amount, grow more life-weight, increase or decrease animals' fertility. According to Baggara cultural knowledge, *um racho* is the least desirable to Baggara rangers, though, it is desirable to their animals, which means Baggara cultural wisdom goes against their animals' taste for this grass; *Um racho* yields less milk and life-weight, and decreased fertility. *Um Chir* ranked among the highest in terms of the above characters. Furthermore, Baggara know the habitat types in which such desirable species grow: *Um chir* grass grows on alluvial soil; *ab asabae* grass grows on laterite (*Gardud*) soil; *Lusieg* grass grows on sandy soil (*Goz*).

Baggara utilize their cultural knowledge about which species is desirable or undesirable, to monitor the environmental changes; if they see *Doctyloctenium aegyptium (ab asabae)* grass replaced by *Tribulus terrestris* (*dirésa*), they change their grazing location which gives the rangeland a chance to recuperate it is nutrient, to allow desirable species reappear. In many cases, the undesirable grasses succeed to replace desirable species permanently; Baggara usually detect this early before moving from one place to another by sending a reconnaissance team (locally called *rawagha*) to survey the area to inform the camps leaders to take action.

Zornia golchidiata (locally called: *lusieg*), is a legume, short herbaceous grass; it is proved extremely dangerous in causing cattle bloating early during the growth season; the grass can cause heavy loses to cattle due to bloat or by causing sheep disease. Building on their transhumance experience, Baggara developed local cultural means from their environment to deal with the grass. During morning times, they allow animals to graze on *lusieg* grass, while during evening time move them to graze on other grasses; sometimes, if bloating is sever they open the cow mouth and pour in hot water and butter; other times they punch open the cow rumen to evict the gases out. Most noteworthy, Baggara allow cows to stand still without moving around for some time until the cows belch the gases. Although the cause of bloating in cattle known for a long period, but, Baggara know only that *zornia* species cause bloat, and they know how to deal with it in most cases.

Although Baggara historically used vegetation to treat diseases, purify drinking water, making perfumes or, as aphrodisiac means, but their knowledge and use of vegetation for environmental purposes have helped them to survive and to succeed in high savannah region.

Table 4: Some herbaceous species that considered desirable for livestock – by Ahmed S. El Wakeel, et. al (1993)

The Scientific name	Vernacular name	Family name
Blerpharis linarifolia	Beghail	Acanthaceae
Brachiaria obtusiflora	Um chir	Gramineae
Chloris prieruri	Abu malih	" "
Doctyloctenium aegyptium	Ab asabae	" "
Echinocloa pyramidalis	Follah	" "
Hyparrhenia confinis	Um racho	" "
Ipomea spp.	Hantoot	Convolvulaceae
Rottboellia exaltata	Um ballilah	Gramineae
Ryncosia minima	Erg al azrag	Papilionaceae
Schizachyrium exile	Um hemeroon	" "
Setaria incrassate	Um sikina	" "
Sorghum purpureo-sericeum	Bigil	" "
Spermacoce chaetocephala	Garagoub	Rubiaceae
Zornia golchidiata	Lusieg	Papilionaceae

STARS AND CELESTIAL OBJECTS:

Nature has given Baggara numerous indicators to theorize when and where the rainy season starts or stops. Among their best indicators are stars: such as the *Greater Bear* (locally called: *Giraffe*), the *Pleiades* or *Messier* (locally called: *Thuraya*' and, the *Milky Way Galaxy* (locally called: *Majara*), and as usual the Sun and the Moon. Baggara have developed a distinct form of Astrology – euphemistically, could be known as Eco-Astrology through which they link between movements and positions of celestial objects and the occurrence of rains and events of the rainy season. Although few astrologers believe that movements and positions of celestial bodies can directly influence life on the Earth or correspond to events experienced on a human scale (from Wikipedia), Baggara, however, have strong believe in their own version of Astrology. They take it for granted that once the movement and position of certain stars corresponds to their presumed believe they act immediately according to that believe to avert themselves the consequence of events.

The *Greater Bear*, which known locally to them as *Giraffe* - should not be confused with the well-known constellation of *Camelopardalis* which also known to the Arabs Astrologers as the *Giraffe* - is of enormous significance to Baggara movement. This constellation is visible in far distant north to the Baggara around the Equator. Among the many asteroids of the *Great Bear*, Alkaid – the leader – is the most valuable one. In Baggara terms, *Alkaid* is known as the head of a giraffe (in Arabic Raas el Zarafa). If "the head of the giraffe" is pointing downward, they say: 'The giraffe has been eating dry grasses", this means it is a midsummer, where trees shed of their leaves and grasses dry out and, their animals will grow weaker from lack of fodder. It also means that they have to search for alternative feeding supplements such sesame cake, cotton cake, or cutting tree branches of semi-deciduous trees such as *Banalities* to feed their animals. This is an exceptionally hard times for Baggara people. However, Baggara are not yearning to know much about "the Giraffe head" when it is down; for them things are clear: watering of animals from wells, feeding, caring about old animals and as such.

The movement of "the Giraffe head" upward is also of considerable significance; it allows them to monitor how far they have been at any moment of time from the rainy season. When "the Giraffe head" is upward, it is for them means heavy rains, which impede their movement to get out of the high savannah region before entrapped by insects. Baggara should move out of the high savannah region way before the "the Giraffe head" stand upright. When "the head of Giraffe" is pointing upward, Baggara say it is eating green shoots; when it is pointing downward, it is eating dry grasses.

The *Milky Way Galaxy* (locally called *Majara*) is of exceptional value for Baggara nomads to know when rainfall is steady and when it is time to move in their transhumance movement northward during the rainy season. Of immense importance is when the asteroids form clear path running south to north; this south-north path for Baggara represents their transhumance route (locally called *morhal*). Baggara, culturally, inclined to believe that God has shown them the route is open for them to move. They usually say, "God has straightened our way". Such cultural inclination proves that Baggara are yearning to know more about the meteorological and weather conditions. Baggara, however, usually, move before the *Milky Way Galaxy* aligns south-north, since this situation means heavy rainfall, which seriously disrupt their movement due to mud and flooding of water valleys; it also subject them to harmful insects outbreak, which my lead to escape of their animals.

During the time of expectation of when rains start or stop, the *Pleiades (Thuraya)* present themself as the most valuable stars. The *Pleiades* have two key positions: when they appear from east and when they disappear at west. Both appearance and disappearance of the *Pleiades* happens just after sunset. Baggara have immense admiration for the *Pleiades* for their glistering splendor. The great benefit to Baggara comes from the ideal correspondence of the *Pleiades* disappearance toward the west just after sunset and appearance from the east just after sunset, which respectively correspond well with the beginning and ending of the rainy season. Baggara have an old saying: "if you see the *Pleiades* disappear just after sunset, fetch a cover for your family from rains and if you see the *Pleiades* appear just after sunset, fetch water-carrying utensils for your family". This indicates how the *Pleiades* engraved in the Baggara cultural consciousness. Since Baggara are nomads, water-carrying utensils in the dry season and cover from rains during the rainy season are vital to their survival. Baggara use the phrase: "fetch water-carrying utensils for your family" to indicate ending of the rainy season and beginning of the dry season, while the phrase: "fetch a cover for your family" means rainy season has started, and families need a shelter from rains.

Baggara, like other early civilizations, know and have greater admiration for Venus (Sudanese vernacular name *ez Zahara*). Many civilizations through history have known Venus, some of them have even worshiped it; the Greeks and the Romans worshiped it as Aphrodite - Goddess of love and beauty; the Babylonians named it Ishtar; the Arabs know it as Uzza - the largest idols in pre-Islamic Arabia. Venus, also, known as the morning star, or the evening star for it is brilliance and luster in those two times.

Baggara, specifically, known Venus as the morning star for its appearance as crystal clear sighting during the early morning hours and stays until about sunrise. Whenever Baggara see Venus on the early hours, they wake up, start their morning prayer, hush their animals to the grazing fields during summer times or, they go to watering places to start pulling water for their animals. During summer times, Venus sets the tone for the day for Baggara activities. When Venus appears toward the east rains stop, and it is only occasionally rains happen after Venus appears from the east, and such rains considered invaluable, since they lead to regrowth and sprouts of grasses during early summer. Baggara used to say, "If rains come after Venus appears, then, it is a lucky year for cattle".

The Moon is one of the invaluable celestial objects. It is importance to Baggara livelihood in savannah remoteness already identified, however, the Moon importance as environmental events predicator are numerous, especially during harvesting season and war times. If a new moon appears as half a ring and phasing upright, Baggara assume a bad harvesting season. If a new moon appears slightly inclined to the south, Baggara assume a successful harvesting season; a north-inclined new moon means a war is possible or bad events maybe inevitable. One of considerable indication of heavy rainfall, locally called *Tarfa*, comes during no-lunar days late on July and late on August each year. Across the Sudanese cultural diversity, Sudanese know the importance of the *Tarfa* for nomads and agriculture. When the *Tarfa* comes, Baggara, usually stop their moving and pass all the *Tarfa* duration in one place. To avoid landlocked by flooding or mud, Baggara usually move to open and accessible places before the *Tarfa* can starts.

The Sun is the greatest and the most invaluable celestial object on the universe, and it is rightly so for the Baggara nomads. Seasons result from the tilt of the Earth's axis relative to the plane of its revolution around the sun, resulting in different parts of the Earth oriented towards the Sun at different times of the year; the tilting - toward or away from the Sun - gives the four seasons of the year - spring, summer, autumn (fall) and winter. The Equator latitudinally divides the Earth in two equal hemispheres: the northern and southern hemispheres. When the northern hemisphere receives a direct sunlight, then it is summer times, while the southern hemisphere is in winter and vice versa. Baggara country falls right about the Equator, which results in a maximum exposure to direct sunlight yearlong. High exposure creates exceptionally hot and dry weather. Evaporation of water and transpiration by trees are at their peak almost throughout the year. Once the rainfall stops, the evaporation leads to dry out of water pools, while transpiration leads to trees shed off their leaves and grasses dry immediately after the rainy season; all these create an unusually harsh weather with limited water resources and pasture for Baggara nomads. To survive such as a hot weather, Baggara dress in a large and wide cloths allowing free air circulation and conserving their bodys' temperature, and water. They adapt their diet to the weather with the least amount of oil in their food during summer time.

Baggara have used stars, the Sun, the Moon and other celestial objects for centuries to monitor what events occurring in their environment, and they used the environment triggers to adjust to their environmental conditions.

7 BAGGARA MATERIAL CULTURES

General Background:

Material culture is the physical evidence of people culture in the objects, things, and architecture that they make, or have made (see Material Culture, Wikipedia 2014). Baggara's material culture emphasizes their unique sense of doing things in their own way, such as building domes, crafting artworks, fashioning costumes, preparing kitchen utencils, making water carriers, braiding their hair, their arms and tools, their cuisine, and many more. Some common themes or factors drive their unique material culture. The first factor among such factors is their liefestyle, which is dependent on nomadism. Nomadism requires agility of movement, and lightweight, rust-free as well as sturdy materials. Lightweight is an important trait for many of Baggara's material things such as mats (*broosh*), water carriers, kitchen's utensils, sleeping material, and dome's construction materials (mats, fabric and plastic covering). A second factor is their skill to use or to utilize nature's materials such as wood, grasses, clay, and bee's wax, to construct or to prepare most of the material things needed in their daily life routines. A third factor is availability of animals for transport, and availability of dairy products such as milk, whey, butter, meat and leathers. Baggara use dairy products as fast food; it is a usual scene that Baggara women give their kids milk while riding on oxen, or Baggara drink sour milk mixed with water and sugar as soon as they settle in a new place to alleviate hunger or quench thirsty. Baggara fast food culture is evident in preparing of *aish* - porridge from flour and added to it milk right from the milking gourd. As resturants in the West keep fast food materials frozen, on the other hand, Baggara keep food materials powdered and dried. Meat, okra, and spices' powder are usual indgrients in almost every meal. Unlike the fast food in the West, which is laden with chemical additives, greese and fat, Baggara fast food is all natural and oraganic.

Within the context of their environment, Baggara dispose a clear sense of unique material culture. The disposition of their culture is evident in their prestigious horse riding, galloping in the wilderness, building their rounded domes, watering their animals, artful coloration of women bodies with *henna* and their unique ornate accessories, carrying of armries by tribal warriors, convening of courts under large baobab trees, marriage festivities in open spaces, and communal eating habit.

Baggara materials culture has close relationship however, to the environment; it is a culture inseparable from the environment in which it grown, flourished and survived. In Baggara culture, one can easily illicit the intelligent purpose behind how things are done the way they do them. For example, chicken coops made of thin bark of *Acacia nubica* interlaced together to allow aeration; coops have sticking out pegs' ending on the bottom to raise the coops above rains water, or to facilitate pitching at the edges of rope-bed during movement. Another example, conglomeration of perfumes from an assortment of aromatic plants material in different forms such as liquid extracts, puree, powder, chips, or ashes, and other materials such as wax and butter as fixing materials, all added in certain proportion to make a rich aroma. Shoes made from different animal's leather types such as tiger, crocodile, poison, monitor or cow leather. Tiger's leather shoes are prestigous and pricy, while cow's leather flip-flop-style shoes are equally cheap as shoes made from used vehicles' tires. Tires shoes are cheap, studay and valuable during raining times. Medications from local herbal plants and the way they serve them or treat aliments are unique and inline with their attitude of using nature.

Agility of Baggara movement from one to another and their need to cover long distance early during the day before sun heat becomes an impeding factor are major factors behind Baggara keeping limited number of items, which are limited to only valuable items. There are no many sets of dishes, cups or pair of clothing. Baggara use of items for multipurposes reduces the overall load and the space required to accommodate the items. The same gourd used for milking also used as eating dish or for drinking water. The mat "*birsh*" used as sleeping mat also used as mat for giving salt to animals or used as shelter from rain. As Swiss Army knife is used as multipurpose tool such as can opening, cutting and ugering, Baggara household items and tools are used similarily for multipurposes. Baggara hammer for example is used to fix nails or remove them from shoes or wood, at the same times used to make bed-ropes (*anagreep*), to make saddles or to hallow trees' trunk to make drums. Agile Baggara movement is evident in their slim body statue. It is very rare to find a fat and slow moving Baggara man or woman in their natural ranges. Culturally, it is not acceptable to be fat or slowly moving. The slim statue of Baggara body is a product of the nature of their food as well as an adaptation to the agile nature of their movement. Baggara are well known for their high activity and quickness of their pace. A crowd of Baggara moving through a forestland easily noticed for how many people leap over stones, rotten woods or water dishes. Instead of waddling across little streams, Baggara can thurst themselves to the other side by jumping over or grapping branches and swinging over the streams. By virtue of their little body statue, Baggara material culture is of lightweight and small-sized items.

Baggara material culture emphasizes the "do-it-yourself" culture, which is most prevailent on the West. A Baggara man does everything by himself. If he does not know how to do something, he will not ask someone to do it for him but rather asks someone to show him how to do it. A Baggara man makes rope-beds, makes hobbles and reigns, digs wells, rafts his water carrier from animal's skin, and tames his ox, horse, donkey or camel. Baggara man grows crops, medicates or gives salts to his animals, and knows the intricate details of the environment in which he lives. Similarly, Baggara women embrace the "do-it-yourself" attitude even to a greater extend than men. Women build domes, prepare meals, milk cows, do artworks and leatherworks, circumsize, be midwife, parter milk products for crops and make mats. They tend crops, create perfumes, gather wild okra, and tap tree barks for domestic purposes. Although in modern society, people tend to special in their profession, on the other hand, Baggara try to know every nauces of their society.

Ingenuity of Baggara ancestors lead to discorvery or invention of materials from or in harmony with their local environment. Although discovery of things might come by observations or trials and errors in the beginning, eventually Baggara developed exceptional talents and skills to deal with or to use nature.

BUILDING BAGGARA DOMES:

Although seem primitive and simple, Baggara domes have intricate structure. The easiest way to grasp how Baggara build domes is to consider the domes composed of three distinct structues: the outer frame, the inner structures namely *rahal* (stacking place), *dranagal* (sleeping place) and *um shalokha* (hanging place) in addition to a little living space.

Baggara usually build rounded domes, which are semi-globular. They are build from trees' branches and saplings. Saplings inserted in holes arranged in a circular fashion and bended inwards and tied together. Spaces between saplings are cress-crossed by smaller saplings and branches, and covered by mats made from *doum palm* (*Hyphaene thebaica*) leaves and some grasses. Mats locally called *Broosh* (sing. *birish*). During summer times, Baggara replace mats with grasses and reeds. Many trees used for building Baggara domes: *Terminalia* spp. (*subagh, subagha*), *Ziziphus spina-christi* (*sider* or *nabbag*), *acacia mellifera* (*kitir*), *Acacia nubica* (*um efana, laot*), banboo, *Cordia spp* (*andrab* or *gambil*), *Grewia tenax* (*guddaim*) and others. Once Baggara settle from their journey in a new place, women rush to find the sticks and saplings that where left over by other Baggara who camped in the area before. If no old structure found, women go to cut new saplings and branches. Usually unwed girls and young girls first job to do after settling is to fetch drinking water from water pools and then go about bringing the branches and saplings. Women go for firewood to start the fire to cook the tea and food. The tea is the first thing to cook and to serve to men within the first hour and half of the Baggara camp settlement in the new place. After women serve tea, food served next; the order of serving tea first then food is a norm in Baggara culture. Once Baggara men finish eating, everyone on the camp goes about his job, including women who are now free to build the domes.

Before women build the dome, a *rahal*, which is stacking structure, is build first to stack the household items. The *rahal* built of six, four-foot long sticks called *sibey*, which grouped in two groups; each group composes of three sticks joined together forming a tripod structure or a triangle with a base of 60 degrees. The base of the front triangle faces the base of the hinter triangle. Two rods connect the two groups of tripods. A long rope runs between the rods forming a net, where household items placed. Structure of rahal can be of bamboo sticks, *Cordia sinensis* (*andrab*), *Albizzia amara* (*arrad*), and *Ziziphus spina-christi* (*sider*). Looking from outside the dome entrance, the *rahal*, always, found on the right side of the dome; it holds the household items such as grains, flour, bags of dates, bag of cloth and everything else need to be up from the ground in order not to be wet if rains water washes through the dome. *Rahal's* sticks carried as part of the household items when journeying from one place to another.

On the far end away from *rahal*, a second structure called *um shalokha* has to be built next. *Um shalokha* serves two purposes: a hanging place for folded clothes and a stacking place for unused mats (*broosh*). *Um shalokha* composes of two y-shaped sticks of equal hight as *rahal's* sticks. The two y-shaped sticks (pl: *shi'ab um shalokha*, sing. *shi'eby*) run parallel to *rahal's* connecting rods; the front *shi'eby* has to be on the same line as the front *rahal's sieby* and rear one has to be on the same line as the rear *rahal's sieby*. A single rod passes through the y-shaped place of the sticks (passes through the y-shaped place of *shi'ab um shalokha*). Usually unused mats stacked on the outer-side of the *um shalokha* away from the *rahal* side, while clothes are folded on the inner-side. *Um shalokha* sticks can be of any wood from any tree, but most women use *Cordia sinensis* (*andrab*) trees and they carry them along their journey from one place to another.

The third structure to be built is a *drangal* – it is a sleeping bed for a family. It runs from *rahal* side to *um shalokha* side; it fills all the space in between them. It is built of nine short v-shaped sticks (pl: *shi'ab el drangal*, sing. *shi'eby*) arranged in three rows of three – it is a three by three structure. The distance between *rahal* and *um shalokha* called the *drangal's* length, and it is always longer than the width from front to back of the *drangal*. Always three long rods run on the top of the v-shaped sticks from *rahal* side to *am shalokha* side through the length of the *drangal* – these long rods called *amaad* (sing. *amood*). The *amaad* (also called *a'ameda*) always selected from a neat material, such as bamboo wood, and permanently kept as part of the family items; they kept during migration. On the top of *amaad* other rods placed, which are running from front to back, these are called *hawadir*. The *hawadir* can be six or nine depending on the family size. Like *amaad*, *hawadir* kept permanently during migration and of the same wood as *amaad*. On the top of *hawadir*, always come *rassas* – a *rassas* is a group of thin sticks about twelve or more; they are placed on the top of the *hawadir* and run in the same direction as of *amaad* and perpendicular to *hawadir*. *Rassas* is also always kept during migration, and it is material is either bamboo or *Acalypha neptunica* (*tuka*) trees or similar soft wood. On the top of the *rassas*, there is another permanent structure, also, called *drangal*, with exactly similar name as the *drangal* already described. This *drangal* is particularly special structure, and always, prepared for a bride by her mother, before moving into her husband quarter – hence, the *drangal* inherited from the bride's family and will continue to exist through the family life unless burnt.

Ali S. Hamouda (2004) described the *drangal* in Hawazma tribes of Baggara as follow: "once the wedding of a bride approaches, her mother built for her the *drangal* (called *sarir*, bed). *Sarir* considered one of the most valuable items awarded to the bride by her mother before moving into her husband dome. *Sarir* always built from bamboo wood sliced in thin slices and weaved together by a thin thread of goat or deer's skin; there are 600 smoothed bamboo slices to make up a single *sarir*. Dimensions of a sarir length measured in arm length (from elbow to the tip of an open palm); *sarir's* length runs six arm length as described above plus one spread of palm (hand stretched from thumb to the middle finger) and *sarir's* width runs three arm length plus one spread of palm (hand stretched from thumb to the middle finger). Both men and women join in preparing and sewing together the drangal". Although Hawazma's *sarir* might not be typical to all other Baggara, but structurally can be representative of all Baggara's *sarir* building and tradition. Ali S. Hamouda (2004) showed the images of *sarir* presented.

During sleeping, a decorated mat covers the *drangal*, and leather billows or normal billows are used.

Always there is a considerable space between the *drangal* and the entrance; this space used as cooking place during raining times and used by the husband or grown boys during night times to house-in their rope-beds.

Once *rahal*, *um shalokha* and *drangal* are in place – the internal structure - then the dome's outer frame is ready to be built around them.

The dome composes of fourteen main and many minor structures; there are six key long main poles called *garanat* (sing. *garan*). One of the six *garanat* is to be fixed on the outer side of the *rahal* and bended inward to join another *garan* coming from *am shalokha* side. Two of the remaining four *garanat* run from the front of the dome forming the entrance to join the two others running from the rear side of the *drangal*. There are other eight main structures called *zaragat* (sing. *zarag*) added to support the dome structure. The *zaragat* joined in similar way to *garanat*, one from one side joined to another from the other side, but run at a lower level as follow: two joined above the entrance and lower to where the *garanat* joined; two joined on the hind side similar to the front *zaragat* in a parallel direction. The other four, run in a similar fashion but on the sides of the dome arching perpendicularly to the previous four *zaragat*. Once the dome frame is in place, then smaller branches, saplings and twigs all together called *carbab*, are cress-crossed to fill in the gaps between the main supporting structures.

Domes covering by mats come as the next step. Usually there are two types of mats: 1) External mats: are coverings of the dome and include outer top mat (called *shouga*), the front mat (called *berish ab khashoum*), which makes the entrance, the back mat (called *berish ab joggie*) and two side mats (called *kattalat*, sing. *kattal*). 2) Internal mats: are decorating mats used to hide the wooden frame of the dome and make it more like a villa's decorated wall -paper and dry walls. There are six of them: three large ones (*shouga*), two side ones (*kattalat*), one inner front and one from inner rear (called *hajalat*, sing. *hajala*).

There is another structure added to the front of the dome on both sides from the entrance called *el tash*. *El tash* is a bark of *Bauhinia rufescens (kharoub)* tree, tapped and peeled in one large chunk, smoothed by pounding the hard outer crust, and then retted in water pools for around one week to remove chemical components. Baggara use retting process for many things including ropes and some types of ryhzomes or underground roots used for food. Unretted tash has short lifespan, hard and rigid to bend. *El tash* originally made to serve a different purpose as an under part of oxen's saddles to form a cushion to distribute the load. When the oxen offloaded, the *tash,* then, used as front covering on the side of the dome entrance. The *tash* also used as an absorpant to sit on for new delivered women and babies. There are seven pieces of *tash* placed on each side of the entrance.

Usually the dome covered with a plastic sheet (called sing. *mashamaa, pl. mashamaat*) to prevent rains from dripping in side, and terraced to prevent water from sweeping in the dome. The plastic sheet can be of any color: blue, white, green, yellow, colored etc.

Finally, the completed dome is covered with a sheet (a cloth sheet called *tagga*). The *tagga* serves two purposes to decorate the dome and fix the plastic sheet in place in order not to be torn off by winds.

Baggara built different types of domes depending on the season; domes covered with grasses are characteristics for summer times while domes covered with mats are characteristic of the rainy season. Domes have different names such as *jahouba, tukul, houmar*.

Inside the dome, the family sleeps in a certain order. A husband usually sleeps either on the far left or far right - he sleeps either next to *drangal* or next to *um shalokha;* a wife separates her husband from kids. The kids sleep according to their ages – the youngest one next to his mother and the eldest one is the farthest away from his mother. Men can also use rope-beds (pl. *anagreeb* sing. *angareb*) for sleeping and sitting. They place their *anagreeb* in front of *drangal* either horizontally or perpendicularly if space permits. Grown up boys, those of ages about seven years old and up, sleep outside the dome, mostly, under trees in the middle of where cows quartered. Girls, including married ones but not yet moved to their husbands domes, sleep inside the family dome until they get marry and move to their husbands place. If a family has a grown up daughter, mostly the husband uses a rope-bed to sleep outside and in front of the dome and only moves in if necessary.

Baggara dome has some extension outside the dome; among them are the *el Drangeil* (*dranjeil*), *el housh*, *el tindil*, *rakoba*, which are explained next.

EXTENSIONS TO BAGGARA DOMES:

1. El drangeil or El sagrdy: is a small thatched extension place to hold the family kitchen's utensils such as pans, pots, and cups. The utensils are placed on the *drangeil* high up from the ground to saveguard them against dogs and other animals. *Drangeil* also serves another purpose, to hold prepared dishes before taken away to *dara* (the communal eating-place); during Fasting (Ramadan) month, women prepare meals and put them up on *drangeil* until about sunset before been carried to *dara* place.

2. El housh: is a fence around the dome, and in numerious times, it is just a demarcation of an area around the dome. The demarcation is done by weeding grasses and cutting off small saplings from the area. Mostly Baggara do not use fences around their dome only during some time of the year, either during the rainy season or during summer times. In Sudanese traditional culture, *el housh* delineates the territory of the property and the ownership; it is just like a wall on cities. Baggara take the *el housh* seriously as a territory, and any stranger who intrudes on *el housh* considered a trespassing and transgressing against the family; such trespassing challenged by the family.

For Baggara, *el housh* serves an important cultural purpose; a clean and large *housh* considered a positive sign for a family wealth, neatness and prestigue. Durinng marriages, women from a groom side visit a bride's family and inspect the *el hush* and surrounding area. Large, neat and orderly *housh* is a welcoming sign for a prospective groom and his family.

3. El Tindil: is a place where Baggara throw the household wastes or sweep the dirt of the dome. Usually, Baggara throw their household wates in one place during sedentary times, especially during summer, winter and rainy seasons. There are cultural elements associated with the appearance of *el tindil* (dirt pile) near the Baggara dome. Large pile of household's dirt considered as sign of family affluence and at the same time considered as sign of cleanliness of the dome. A family, which has nothing, produces no dirt and their *tindil* is by definiion does not exist.

4. El Terrace: Terrancing is a well-known agricultural practice in Africa and elsewehere on mountaineous areas farms. The farmers tilt the soil in a form of series of narrow ridges down the slope to hold water for enough times to irrigate their crops. Baggara use similar terracing technique by digging a single ditch around the dome to keep water run-off out of their domes. By making Terrance, Baggara ensure that floodwater not sweeps through the domes and carry off their belonging unknowlingly. Baggara women dig up the ditch around the dome and push the digged up soil against the dome base and smoothe out the outer part of the ditch to ease the water run-off.

Mats as Cultural Items:

Baggara are traditional mats makers. Mats locally called *broosh* (sing. *berish*) made from either the date palm (*Phoenix dactylifera*) leaves or doum palm (*Hyphaene thebaica*) leaves, but Baggara make the mats exclusively from doum palm's leaves. Women are sole makers of mats in the Baggara communities. Culturally, all nomadic Baggara women are mats' makers. A Baggara woman, who does not know how to make mats like a woman who does not know how to cook; this fact has significant drawback on her image and self-esteem as a wife, and may jeopardises chances of her daughters as future wives. Baggara women are highly artistic mats' makers. They produce very fine quality and grades of mats with intriguing designs and decorations for domestic use and marketing purposes. Baggara women learn how to craft and to design mats at young ages, and without any schooling. Learning mats making is part of Baggara girls early childhood's home schooling by their mathors ad grandmothers. Baggara girls start learning mats making by making simple, common purpose mats and as they get skilled gradually moved into a more complex designs until they reach the point to envision their own designs and exeute them. Mothers take pride in teaching their daughters to make mats and to cook.

Baggara use mats for varying purposes. Such use includes: a) covering for the domes, b) a sleeping material just as matrices, c) sitting on material like any mat but especially during festivities or death, d) salting animals – when salting animals, the salt placed on the mat on the rope-bed, e) covers from rains, f) prayer mats – just like prayer rugs or carpets, and g) carrying deceased persons.

Mats are usually made of varying sizes and shapes. Smaller mats used as sleeping mats or for daily use purposes. Large mats used to cover the domes or decorate them from inside. Women decorate mats in two ways: by dying sun-dried, leaves with a dye, or by using a grass locally called *hireira* by overlaying it on the leaves to make them look shinny. Decorated mats used as insulators and as decorative inside the domes, to hide the structure of the dome's frame from sight or they used to cover wedding domes during marriage celebration. Decorated mats also used for guests but never used for salting animals – for the later purpose, Baggara use a normal white mat.

Mats types have different names: a) Shouga, b) Kattal c) Kattal ab khasoum, d) Ab Joggie (ab joggey), e) Haggal (Hajala), f) Berish ab khashoum g) Berish el drangal (large sleeping mat), h) Berish el salah (prayer mats), i) Berish el Noum (small sleeping mats), and i) Mufrasha (sitting on mat). Mats names are significant for Baggara. Once the name of the mat is known, Baggara then know what quality of material is used for making them and what the purpose of the mat is. Mats types from a) *Shouga* up to f) *Berish ab khasoum* are introduced earlier under the internal and external covering of the domes; the rest of mats types are self-explanatory.

ROPES AS CULTURAL ITEMS:

Traditionally, Baggara are ropes makers. Ropes play important roles in Baggara culture; they are used for fasting luggage, pulling water from wells, reigning animals, hobbles and many more. Baggara males - young or old - know how to make ropes. The traditions of ropes making dated back to the old good days when Baggara ancestors lived isolated in wilderness and had no access to urban centers to buy industrial ropes. The traditions of ropes making carried on because of the fact that materials used for ropes making are available for free from the natural environment where Baggara live. Baggara make many types of ropes for different purposes. Generally, ropes used for carrying loads, tieing baggage together, fastening mats, attaching utensils, hobbles, and reigns. Everything loaded on an animal, somehow, fastened to the rest of the load by a rope.

Baggara make ropes from different sources, however, mostly they made them from trees' barks or some herbaceous plants' fibers. Among the most used trees, is baobab tree (*Adansonia digitata*, Sudanese vernacular name; *tabaldi*). Barks of a baobab tree peeled off and used to make ropes. Mostly the Baggara ret the ropes or barks in retting water in order to make ropes. Baggara also use Corchorus *Corchorus olitorius* (Sudanese vernacular name: *malokhia*) and *Corchorus capsularis* (Sudanese vernacular name: karang). *Corchorus* harvested by cutting the plants at or close to the ground level. Next, the plants tied into bundles and the branching tops lopped off. The bundles placed side by side in retting water, usually in 2 to 3 layers and tied together. They are covered with mud inside the water pool. The endpoint determined by inspecting a few plants each day from the tenth day onwards. If fiber slips out easily from the wood on pressure from the thumb and fingers, retting considered complete.

Types of Baggara Ropes:

a) Zimil for handling bulky loads.

b) Salab similar to zimil.

c) Zomam it is a reign for ox, passed through the nose of a tame ox.

d) Rasan it is a reign for camels.

e) Gournat for milking cows, one tied on the cow rear legs and one for tying the calf to the front leg.

f) Ouglat (sing. Ougal) means hobbles for tying the camel leg when lay on the ground.

g) Gayed (pl. goyoud) hobbles for shackling camel front legs or donkey two legs: one front and one rear.

h) Um shababa is rope, which is tied to the head of unruly cow to catch her for milking.

i) Ripig it is rope for tying many calves together in a single rope.

j) Habil el Eigal it is rope for tying a calf to a wood or a tree.

k) Shabaka it is a network placed, around the mouth of a young calf, to prevent him from suckling.

l) Wajaj it is rope made either of leather or from the fiber of the stem of doum palm's leaves.

m) Nisaah is rope made from either leaves of doum palm or leather by braiding as in hair braiding.

n) Tujaj it is a coiled rope used to make rope-beds.

   Baggara also use animal's skins to make ropes.

BEDS AS CULTURAL ITEMS:

As in cases of mats and ropes, Baggara are traditional rope-beds (*anagreeb*) makers. Baggara men exclusively make rope beds; women rarely make rope beds. Rope-bed composes of different parts. Baggara beds made from wood of various trees; different parts of the bed may come from different tree species. Bed legs usually obtained from: *Prosopis Africana* (Sudanese vernacular name: um surouj), *Balanites* *aegyptiaca (haglig)*, *Ceratonia siliqua (kharoub)*, *Anogeissus leiocarpus (sahab)*, *Ficus sycamorus (gumez)*, *Lannea fruticosa (leon)*, *Lannea spp (milays)*, *Sclerocarya birrea* ssp. *(humied)*, *Acacia gerrardii (salgum)*, etc. The rest of the structure of bed comes from any trees that have sturdy enough wood to support the weight. Namely *hawadir –* the long rods connecting the legs can be from *Acacia seyal (talh)*, *Balanites aegyptiaca (haglig)*, *Tamarindus indica (aradeib)*, *Cordia sinensis (andrab)*, *Terminalia* spp. *(subagh, subagha)*, *Prosopis Africana (*Sudanese vernacular name: um surouj)*, *bamboo*, *Albizzia amara (arrad)*, *Ziziphus spina-christi (sider)*, etc.   *Wasayid* – the short rods connecting legs can from the same trees from which *hawadir* made or from different trees, since they obtained from trees which short wood. Rope beds' net material are mostly from ropes made from the doum palm or *Corchorus* (*Corchorus olitorius*, Sudanese vernacular name: *malokhia*) and *Corchorus capsularis* (Sudanese vernacular name: *karang*).

There are different types of anagreeb for different purposes:

a) *Angareb kabir* – large bed, for sleeping, it is a general purpose *angareb*

b) *Gaad* – for sitting, also called (*ab'jeabey*), also used for kids as sleeping bed and young born

c) *Banbar* – small bed exclusively used by women when cooking or chatting.

d) *Angareb el khoumam* - this is a special *angareb,* used by young ladies, and brides, to show off their luggage, during migration or when the brides move to her husband's dome.

HOUSEHOLD UTENSILS AND TOOLS:

Household items and utensils can include cooking pots, cans, pans, dishes, cups, stone grinder (*mourhaka*), gourds (*garaa*), stoves, tea kettles, coffee kettles, milk gourds, calabashes, and other milk carrying utensils (*garaa*), leather's water carrier (*sien*); images at the end of this chapter show part of the dome utensils.

Some names are below:

1. Laban: milk.
2. Mouya: water
3. Bukhasat el laban: calavash for holding milk.
4. Am kung: metallic pot.
5. Hallah: can.
6. Dowka: clay pot or clay pan.
7. Morhaka: stone grinder.
8. Al muswat: porridge-stirring stick.

126

9. Al ladaya: three stones to hold the pots while cooking.
10. Kouz: metallic cup used for drinking water.
11. Kubaya: tea cup.
12. Funjal: coffee cup.
13. Kas: gourd.
14. Kafaterah: boiling water can with a top handle.
15. Barad: tea pot.
16. Jabana: coffee pot.
17. Shargrag: coffee pot.
18. Shaghal: same as Shargrag.
19. Sahan: dish
20. Maalaga: spoon.
21. Gaddah: wooden dish.
22. Al Saj: metallic flat pan.
23. Jagg: a pot for milk, juice or water.
24. Mougrafa: porridge scope.
25. Kisra: flat sheet of porridge.
26. Gargaraiba: a piece of daleib (*Borassus aethiopum*) leave used to stir Kisra.
27. Aish: porridge.
28. Aish el laban: porridge served with milk.
29. Al moulah: sauce
30. Gerba: skin water carrier.
31. Sien: skin water carrier, smaller than Gerba.
32. El gesh: grass.
33. El hatab: fire wood or building wood.
34. Al mukhraz: peg.
35. Al misala: large needle.
36. Al shakoush: hammer.
37. Gadada: chisel.
38. El fas: an axe.
39. Mouhfar: ground digging tool.
40. Atala: lever.
41. Hashasha: weeding tool.
42. Satour: machete.
43. Sakiin: knife
44. Tujaj: locally made ropes.
45. Soyour: strings of leather, sing. sayr.
46. Dabaya: leather containers, sing. dabyeh.
47. Karayu: basket containers, sing. karyouyeh, also small calavashes.
48. Al najar: wood carpentering tool.

49. Hababa: air fan.
50. Tabag: dish covering.
51. Ttawa: pan.
52. Kanoun: metal mesh stove.
53. Pistilleh: small container.
54. Jardal: large metallic container.
55. Foondog: mortar.
56. Mousfa: sieve.
57. Madaq: small mortar.
58. Yad el Madaq: handle used to pound on the mortar.
59. Moukhbar: Clay Stove used for carrying fire, and used by women during smoke's path.
60. Misraja: kindle for lighting up during dark nights
61. Eipreeg: prayer jar, it is a plastic jars for holding water for abolition.
62. Kowra: metallic pot.

Plate 31: Baggara woman cooking during evening time, showing all need household utensils.

32: Baggara girl cooking tea. Young girls do all domestic homework.

Plate 33: Close lookup - pot, can, cooking stick for stirring porridge in the pots, wire stove, and a large sauce spoon.

Plate 34: Tea cooking kettle sits on Kanun – a Tea Wire Stove.

Plate 35: Teapot, teacups, tray and spoon sitting small table. All these items are part of tea tradition any mishandling is punishable by Baramka.

Plate 36: Coffee kettles, although coffee well-served and received in Baggara communities but it has lower traditions compared to tea.

Plate 37: A Metal Mortar for pounding spices, dried Okra, dried meat and anything need pounding to be added to sauce.

Plate 38: A Wooden Mortar for and iron handle for pounding spices, dried Okra, dried meat and others in order to make a sauce.

Plate 39: Water and milk jars also used for juice during festivities – people can dip their juice cups and dring.

Plate 40: Sieve, knife and other cooking utensils.

Plate 41: This structure is called Drangeil, it is built outside Baggara dome to hold cooking utensils (two stories Drangeil).

Plate 42: Drangeil structure, holding all cooking utensils, used to stack cooking utensils up from animals and kids.

Plate 43: Cooking pot hanged on Drageil structure.

Plate 44: Dishes, tea cups, tea kettles and other carrying water utensils.

Plate 45: Clay Stove used for carrying fire, and also used by ladies during smoke's path. Baggara ladies are fond of smoke's path. Smoke path is used heavily by Sudanese women for body lifting.

Plate 46: Wooden Mortar used for threshing grains or dry okra.

Plate 47: Wooden Mortar characteristic for pounding coffee and dried aromatic plants to make local perfumes.

Plate 48: Baggara kindle for lighting up during dark nights.

Plate 49: Gourd used to hold milk, milk fermentation and separating butter from milk, it is very important item in Baggara household items.

Plate 50: Animal skin jar used for holding water and keeping it cool.

Plate 51: Plastic jars for holding water. Water also holded on animal leathers.

Plate 52: Epreeg – brayer bottle, there are metallic and plastic types.

Plate 53: Dishes and covers. Baggara eat while sitting on the ground.

Plate 54: Decorated mats (*Broosh*), all types of mats are made by women.

Plate 55: Setting on fire early morning using twigs and small pieces of wood. Behind the scene is see how Baggara stretch their washed items.

Plate 56: Slaughtering is exclusively done by men. Baggara hang slaughtered animal on a tree branch usually head down.

Plate 57: Baggara rope-bed style used both as couch and sleeping bed.

a)   Plate 58: Litte rope-bed used by women while cooking or chatting.

8 BAGGARA TRANSHUMANCE: LIFE, MOVEMENT AND COMMUNICATION IN THE WILDERNESS

Baggara are nations on the move. Their life, livelihood and daily routines of households are greatly shaped by nomadic movements from one place to another.

Baggara transhumance life centered on cattle movements and subsistence: where should cattle be moved? How do material things, such as food, secured on the new place? Is there any drinking water in the new place? Are there any diseases? With such straightforward questions, Baggara gather all needed information to move from one place to another. Transportation during movements provided by one own camels, oxen, donkeys or horses. Without bridges or tunnels, nomads cross the rivers using ropes, climbing trees, and muddying through water streams or swimming across a watercourse; if the watercourse is large enough like a river, Baggara will never cross to the other bank; in this case, they limit their activities to the river's bank where it happens to be on their side. There is nothing in their life like televisions, newspapers, Internet, dish networks, air microwaves or movie theaters. Women rarely visit clinics, doctors or health professionals; they deliver at hands of traditional nursesand midwives using traditional equipment such as knifes or razors without any anesthesia or detergents. Millets, bulrush millets, sorghum, and milk are the main staple food; porridge cooked for any meal during the day. Tea is their best drink.

Baggara transhumance life can be thought of as too simplistic, primitive, lacking excitement or just a worthless life. These views shared by travelers who occasionally visit Baggara camps. Yet the truth of the matter is that nomadic and transhumance life is far different from a city or a village life, and comparison in most cases is unlikely; it is a life that stands by its own – full of excitements, happiness, dancing, singing, and chorales (Baggara's *dramaley* dance is one of the best chorals). Horns, stringed instruments (*um kiki* – single string instrument), drums (*nogara*)

143

are among, usual instruments to be heard in the Baggara wilderness.

Baggara have two main movements and two minor movements during the year. The two main movements run south to north (called *tadali*) or north to south (called *mou'wota*) depending on the rainy season; the first one - *tadali* - occurs at the start of rainy seasons where Baggara start to move toward their northern herding season (south to north movement); the other one – *mou'wota* - occurs at the end of the rainy season toward their southern dry season grazing zones (north to south movement). The names *tadali* and *mou'wota* are extremely well-known names across Baggara country. The two minor movements are short movements; one occurs during early rainy season before starting of the *tadali* movement – this short movement called "*rushash*"; the other short movement occurs late, at about the end of *mou'wota* movement – this called "*moushta*". The *rushash* can come under different names such as *noushowq, murshash* etc. These names can be used interchangeably to mean the same thing - *rushash*.

Table 2: Transhumance movements – names, occurrence, and Baggara activities.

Transhumance movement Name	occurrence	Direction of Movement	Activities
Rushash	Early rainy season	Mostly latitudinal	Animals are weak and crumbling, just coming out of the dry season, they need particular care
Tadali	Rainy season	South to north	Animal are healthy, and they need little care.
Mou'wota	Late rainy season	North to south	Animal are healthy, need special care not to break into local people farms
Moushta	End of the rainy season	Mostly latitudinal	A lot of nomads and farmers issues over grazing and water resources.

A DAY IN THE LIFE OF BAGGARA TRANSHUMANCE PERSON:

Baggara have rich customs, tradition and norms while moving from one place to another. There are common activities carried out in almost every time they move from one place to another. All of such activities called *morhal* customs – routes customs or called *masar* or *rahoul* customs

– movement's customs. Following is a brief description of such customs:

RECONNAISSANCE SURVEY (*RUWAGHA*):

One or two days ahead of a camp movement, a person or two sent to do a reconnaissance survey of a new place – this called *ruwagha*. *Ruwagah* is basic for gathering of information about the new place – called *munzala*. The person or persons sent are trustworthy men, who everyone in the camp belief in their sound judgment. The person, who does the reconnaissance called *ruwagh* pl. *ruwaghiin* – surveyors. Usually they ride on horses, donkeys, or camels, to gather information about the *munzala*. When they return, elders question them about their findings. The elders ask them about availability of water and for how long can support the camp; they ask them how diseases, danger, harmful insects and safety of the new place.

Once the *fariq* – camp assured about the new place *munzala* by *ruwaghiin*, the word spread out about the elders intention when should the *fariq* moves to the new place, and everyone should know when they are moving in order his duties during movement day – called *masar* day.

MOVEMENTS (*RAHOUL OR MASAR*):

Rahoul is the act of moving from one place to another also called – *Masar* and *Morhal* (pl. *maraheel or morahiil*). The *morhal* is a route Baggara follow when moving to a new place. Each tribe or group of tribes has one *morhal* to follow, from south to north during *tadali* journey, and another one to follow from north to south during *mou'wota* journey – mostly the same tribe follows only two routes in their transhumance journeys lifelong. Bagara have rich traditions regarding control of movement along the *morhal*; one of such tradition is if two moving camps join the *morhal* at the same time, the one which entered the *morhal* first has to continue their move while the other tribe or camp halts until the last person of the moving tribe passes. If a tribe who previously uses another route – *morhal*, decided to use a different *morhal*, the tribes which have ownership of the *morhal*, may stop them if their animals infected or if they afraid they might create a problem on the *morhal*.

Some Terminologies of Movements

Rahoul: is the Baggara movement from one place to another; it usually implies moving for a short distance.

Masar: is the Baggara movement from one place to another for a longer distance than *rahoul.*

Morhal: is the route Baggara follow when moving from one place to another; mostly each tribe has two *morahiil* ; one for south to north movement and another one for north to south movement.

Munzala: is a new place, where Baggara recently settled (*Manazil* is plural).

Nouzoul: is the act of settling in the new place.

Ratiya: is coagulated sour milk.

Nasia: sour, skimmed milk mixed in water.

Gufas (sing. gafas): cages for carrying chickens from one place to another.

Da'iyyna: is a moving camp.

Dara: men gathering place.

Fariq: the camp.

Fatour: breakfast.

Ghada: lunch.

Asha'a: dinner.

Safayiin: oxen saddles.

Rabita: a roll of mats (pl. *rabayit*).

Abareeg: prayer water bottles.

Evening before Movement Day:

On the evening before transhumance journey (called *masar*), Baggara trumpet a large drum with their signature. Each Baggara tribe or subtribe has its own drum code of informing others, about who they are. Once that signature or code drummed, other people around them take notice of the name of their tribe or subtribe. After the tribe drums out its signature, if it is intention to move tomorrow, it drums the rhythms for movement.

The Morning of *Rahoul* Day:

On the movement day, Baggara start their day early in the morning when roosters start crocking. During times of movement, Baggara grandfathers and grandmothers wake up early, and they start their day by catching chickens before they set off from their sleeping places and pack them in cages (called *gufas*, sing. *gafas*) especially prepared for transporting them. Once the chickens packed, Baggara old men do their morning prayer, and women set on fire, to make morning tea. During this day, everyone, including young boys and girls, waked up early to carry their duties. Girls go to start tearing down Baggara domes and roll the mats together. Boys guard the cattle not to leave the quarter while milking cows with women. Young kids – boys and girls, take care of sheep and goats guarding, and count the chickens if any is missing. Once the sun raises, the men briefly gather on *dara* – a gathering place, to drink their morning tea and eat a little meal called *fatour* – breakfast, mainly of porridge in milk or just they drink sour milk called *ratiya*. Immediately, after morning tea, men lift their rope-beds and they go to their families; they place the rope-beds where they used by women, to load household items and chicken *gufas*. The men occupy themselves in reigning oxen, camels, donkeys and horses and bring them to place where they loaded with the language; they saddle them with saddles (*safayiin*) in case of oxen; saddles donkeys and horses with *sourj* – donkey's saddles; they saddle camels with *hawaya* – saddle for camels.

For each ox or camel to be loaded, there will be two equal-weighed rolls of mats (called *rabayit* sing. *rabita*), each loaded on one side, and the load properly balanced to avoid falling or wounding the oxen or camel. *Rabayit* are nothing but rolls of mats and within them included sticks used to build *draganals* – Baggara beds, or sticks for building *rahal* – a stacking place in the Baggara dome, and sometimes they roll all sticks for building Baggara domes inside the *rabayit*. On the top of the *rabayit*, Baggara hang a lot of stuff including cans, pots, plastic jars, kettles and much more on each side of the load but always keep a well-balanced load.

Young ladies prepare their luggage differently; they do not use large and long rolls of mats instead they use short decorated rolls of mats. The young ladies do not hang stuff on the rolls when loaded on camels or oxen; instead they hang a lot of decorative materials on the bed (called *angareb el khoumam*) made especially for unwed and married young ladies. The young ladies put bells, whistles, horns, ostrich feathers, empty decorated glass bottles, threaded leather strings (called *khoumam*), leather carriers (called *dabaya*, sing. *dabyeh*), and special billows (*wasayid*). The young ladies lavishly decorate their beds where they will not be seen while sitting on them on oxen or camel back, such structure called *khoumam's* bull for unwed ladies or wedding bull for married ladies. The bulls decorated including decorating its horns, placing ostrich fears on its head, decorating its reign, placing see shells beads on its neck or around its horns and decorating everything that can be decorated on the bull. If two or more young ladies ride alongside each other or behind each other in a row on the journey, they create an impression of a caravan full of decorations; people always curiously peek to see who is inside the *khoumam*. The bills will ring all journey long; some of the bills are small ringing continuously while others are large bills making a clucking noise.

Once everything loaded with the exception of bed still on the ground, then one person ask the people on the camp to see if all are ready to lift the beds and put them on the oxen or camels backs. Once they do so, the women ride their oxen and the crowd moves on their journey; cowboys hush the cattle, goats and sheep to move together with moving camp. Nothing will be left behind except smoldering stumps of wood and the dirt of their animals.

Once they move for a short distance, usually they join the main route – called *morhal*, which all tribes share. A leader with a big drum on his ox or camel will trumpet the drum as they move. The animals, lost animals and the crowd understand the essence of the moment that the camp is moving to a new place, and all expeditiously move along. Intermittently, the leader or his assigned person for the drum keeps trumpeting the drum, continuously changing between the tribe signature rhythm and a moving or a reaching destination rhythm. Others settled or moving tribes know who is coming to their vicinity based on the drum rhythms.

REACHING DESTINATION – (EL NOUZOUL):

Once the moving camp reaches the destination, a drum trumpeted to indicate the moving camp (called *da'iyyna*), reaches the destination. Everyone hears the sound of the drum knows about the tribe, which is just has reached its destination. Women spread on wide area, and each chooses a large, well-shaded tree to step off in front of it leaving it on the inward of the *fariq* – the camp. Usually, the camp laid in a circular manner and every woman knows where she should fit in the circle. If a family dome should face westward then everywhere they go, this family stays on the east side of the camp facing west. When each woman determined her location in the *farig*, she steps off from her ox or knees down her camel. Men, immediately, join women and girls to off load the luggage from animals. Cowboys start to separate young calves from their mothers in the herd and give their control to young boys and girls to take care of them for the rest of the day or part of the day until the herds move to the grazing range (called *falah*). Grandfathers and grandmothers get extremely exhausted at the time of reaching the destination and immediately, they take their *anagreeb* (sing. *Angareb* - bedstead) and move under shade trees. All grandfathers in the farig gather under a single shade tree, such as *Tamarindus indica* (*aradeib*), *Adansonia digitata* (*tabaldi*), *Balanites aegyptiaca* (*haglig*), *Albizzia amara* (*arrad*), *Ziziphus spina-christi* (*sider*) or any densely shaded trees. This gathering place called *dara*, and it is where all men, young men and boys eventually gather to drink tea, *nasia* (sour skimmed milk diluted with water) and eat *assiyda* (porridge). Young men direct cowboys where to take the herds for grazing. Thereafter, they occupy themselves with making *zariba* – a place to dome the calves while their mothers in the camp. They gather thorn from old Baggara *dar* (a place where Baggara had earlier quartered and left) or cutting branches from thorny trees such as *Ziziphus spina-christi* (*sider*), *Balanites aegyptiaca* (*haglig*) or *acacia mellifera* (*kitir*).

Women and girls occupy themselves with collecting firewood and bringing water from a nearby water pools or wells. Once they gather the firewood and water, women set on fire, to make tea and *assiyda*. Tea made first and brought to men, where grandfathers gathered; the food served after the tea served – this meal called *ghada* - lunch. Then, women move to collecting sticks and saplings left over from previous Baggara who quartered nearby to the place; if no old material found, they go to a nearby forested area to cut fresh saplings and sticks to build domes (see how they build under: Building Domes on the next chapter).

Little girls and grandmothers much burdened, once *da'iyyna* (the moving camp) reaches its destination, by taking care of young kids and newborns and at same times young girls serve the elderly by bringing water to them or filling their prayer bottles (*abareeg*) and prayer mats (*berish el salah*).

Boys take care of calves, goat, sheep and rear camels near to *farig* – camp.

Once everything settled and everyone took care of his assigned duties, young men start looking for settled people in their vicinity, they communicate with them and gather more news and information about the new place. Old men also carry similar roles by taking to settled people – this called *takhabur*.

THE EVENING OF ENCAMPMENT:

On the evening, around sunset, boys return the calves, goat and sheep to the *fariq* quarter. Calves put in thorn quarters (*zaraib*, sing. *zariba*) awaiting their mothers to come. At sunset, the cowboys bring the herds back to the quarters, and the whole people in the fariq including cowboys indulge in milking the cows. Thereafter men gather in the middle of *fariq* in a place called *dara* – (the gathering place, which now moved from where grandfathers previously gathered under shade trees to the middle of the camp). Women send girls or cowboys to bring food to the *dara*, the meal called *asha'a* – dinner meal. After the *asha'a* meal, men stay for a short time chatting and eventually disperse to go to sleep.

Usually, young men and young girls go for lunar days' dance if it is lunar times or the young men gather by themselves under a tree chatting about girls and women affairs. When they get sleepy, they bring their mats (*broosh*) and sleep on the same spot under trees within cows' quarter in order to guard the cows during night times.

Plate 59: Baggara moving camp (farig) during seasonal journey, women riding on bulls.

Plate 60: Baggara herd moving during seasonal journey.

Plate 61: Baggara wedding dome, covered with colorful mats.

Plate 62: Baggara camp during summer times. Photo courtesy of Rita Willaert.

Plate 63: Baggara dome during the rainy season, although seems unwelcoming from outside, but it is warm and resourceful.

Platte 64: Baggara camp during the rainy season.

Plate 65: Moving Baggara camp (farig) during early summer times.
Photo courtesy of Rita Willaert.

Plate 66: Moving Baggara camp (farig) during early summer times.
Photo courtesy of Rita Willaert.

Plate 67: Moving Baggara camp (*farig*) during early summer times. Baggara use camels, oxen and donkeys during their journey, Photo courtesy of Rita Willaert.

Plate 68: Moving Baggara camp (farig). Girls riding on dokenys. Photo courtesy of Rita Willaert.

Plate 69: Recently settled Baggara camp (farig). Photo courtesy of Rita Willaert.

Plate 70: Recently settled Baggara camp (farig). Girls fetching water. Photo courtesy of Rita Willaert

9 BAGGARA CULTURE: NAMES OF TREES, GRASSES, BIRDS, AND WATER RESOURCES

This chapter is a listing of names and resources on the Baggara zones; it is intended to construct a quick resource reference of what the natural habitats are.

COMMON TREES, SHRUBS AND GRASSES:

Some useful Trees and Grasses used by Baggara for different purposes.

Scientific Names	Baggara Vernacular Names
Adansonia digitata	Tabaldi
Adenium honghel	Shadart El-sim
Acacia albida	Haraz
Acacia ehrenbergiana	Salam
Acacia gerrardii	Salgum
Acacia mellifera	Kitir
Acacia nilotica	Sunt
Acacia nubica	Um Efeana, Laout
Acacia senegal	Hashab
Acacia seyal	Taleh
Acacia siberiana	Kuk
Acacia tortilis	Seyal
Acalypha neptunica	Tuka
Amaranthus viridis	Lissan-tair Kabir
Andropogon gayanus	Aborakhus
Anogeissus leiocarpus	Sahab
Balanites aegyptiaca	Haglig
Bauhinia spp.	Kulkul
Blepharis linarifolia	Bigual
Blerpharis linarifolia	Beghail
Borassus aethiopum	Daleib
Boswellia papyrifera	Tarag-tarag
Brachiaria obtusiflora	Um Chir
Cassia obtusifolia or synonym Senna obtusifolia	Kawal

157

Capparis deciduas	Tundub
Cassia senna	Sanamakah
Cenchrus biflorus	Huskneet
Ceratonia siliqua	Kharoub
Chloris prieruri	Abu Malih
Citrullus colocynthis	Handul
Cleome gynandra	Tamaleka
Combretum spp.	Habil
Commiphora africana	Gafal
Corchorus capsularis	Karkang
Corchorus olitorius	Malokhia
Cordia abyssinca	Gimbil
Cordia sinensis	Andrab
Courbonia virgata	Kirdan
Crateva adansonii	Debkar
Crotalaria saltiana	Sofeira
Cucumis melo var. agrestis	Ajour al rawa'ia
Doctyloctenium aegyptium	Ab Asabae
Dalbergia melanoxylon	Babanus
Dichrostachys cinerea	Kadad
Diosphyros mespiliformis	Jugan
Grewia tenax	Guddaim
Echinocloa colonum	Difra
Echinocloa pyramidalis	Foolah
Ficus sycamorus	Gumez
Heliotropium spp.	Danab Elagrab
Hymenocardia acida	Himeira
Hyparrhenia confinis	Um Racho
Hyphaene thebaica	Dom
Ipomea spp.	Hantoot
Ipomea carnea	Aweer
Lannea fruticosa	Layeon
Lannea spp	Milays
Leptadenia arabica	Um Luweiso
Merremia pinnata	Hantoot
Mimosa pigra	El-Mustahiya
Nerium oleander	Ward elhameir
Oncoba spinosa	Abun Gawi
Parkinsonia aculeata	Sesaban
Phoenix dactylifera	Nakhil

Prosopis Africana	Um Surouj
Rottboellia exaltata	Ab Ballilah
Ryncosia minima	Erg al Azrag
Salvadora persica	Arak
Sclerocarya birrea ssp.	Humied
Stereospermum kunthianum	Khashkhash
Terminalia spp. (subagh, subagha)	Subag
Tribulus terrestris	Diresa (Um Direso)
Ximenia Americana	Um mdeka
Zornia glochidiata	Shilieni or lusieg
Xeromphis nilotica	Shagarat el Murfaein

BIRDS COMMON ON BAGGARA ZONES:

Some Common Birds Encountered by Baggara or Used by them as Environmental Predicators:

Andrea spp	Herons	Habib
Balearica pavonina ceciliae	Crowned Crane	Garnoug
Bubulcus ibis	Egrets	Abou Rahou
Bucorvus leadbeateri	Ground-hornbill	Abun Duluk
Caprimulgus affinis	Nightjar	Um Kititi
Ciconia ciconia	white storks	Simbr, Koljoy
Ciconia nigra	Black storks	
Columba livia	Dove	Dabaz
Gyps africanus	White-Backed Vulture	Um Gadamain
Himantopus himantopus	Black-winged Stilt	Tayr Elmi
Lamprotornis chalybaeus	Greater Blue-eared Starling	Al Akaa
Leptoptilos crumeniferus	Marabou Stork	Abun Kharita
Macrodipteryx vexillarius		Um Kititi or Um al Ri'yan
Merops pusillus	Little Bee-eater	Shinater
Numida meleagris	Helmeted Guineafow	Jidad al Wadi
Oena capensis	Namaqua Dove	Blauwm
Sagittarius serpentarius	Secretary Bird	Sagor El Jidyan

Streptopelia decipiens	Mourning Collared-Dove	Gumeri
Struthio camelus	Ostrich	Na'am
Tockus erythrorhynchus	Toucan	Abu Mangoor
Tockus erythrorhynchus	Toucan	*Abu Mangoor*
Upupa epops, U. senegalensis	hoopoes	Hoodhud, Abun Tagag

COMMON WORDS OR TERMINOLOGIES:

Angereyb: bedstead, a rope-bed.

Atmur: a place has red clay soils with a lot of trees, mostly unthorny.

Awlad: Sons.

Azzaba (azab): not married woman (azab not married man).

Bagar hurrat: cows of the best breed.

Bahr: river.

Baret el suf: a cow given to a newborn when they shave him by the seventh day. Suf means hair. Bara or baret means cow.

Baret el sura: a cow awarded to the child when born.

Bayt: dome or Baggara dome

Dar: land.

Daret: early dry season.

Darangal (dringil): a bed within Baggara dome, built for all family member to sleep together in it.

Dara: place where all men gather to eat and chat.

Dor: cows' place where they sleep.

Eyne: climax of rains.

Fau: cracking clay land which will flooded by rains.

Farig: camp.

Fudda um suf: nickname for cows; fudan means silver; um suf: with hair.

Gardud: noncracking red clay soil.

Gheem: a midge (tabanid family); tiny mosquotoes.

Goz: sandy areas; sand dunes.

Grewa: rough, early dry season's winds.

Hilla: village.

Holie (holia): one year old calf.

Iyal: sons

Jeda (jeda'a): two years old cow.

Junghur shanab el hout: cows are nicknamed by Baggara as fish.

Kartot: little, ill calf.

Kharif: the rainy season.

Kharif bukli:

Kharif bukli: the height of the rainy season; rainy season which has heavy rains.

Khashm el rahad: water pool vicinity.

Khumam: mouth or vicinity.

Madmun (madmuna): more than one year old calf.

Mal: wealth such as cows.

Masikh: lacking taste; tasteless.

Midd: measure for grains (around 16 ounce)

Muglad: land with red clay soil and low vegetation.

Munsalab: young calf.

Munshagh: early rainy season times.

Naga'a: eroded area.

Nazir: paramount chief of the tribe.

Netarda bil mal: chase him away with high dowry money; a form of soft refusal to marry someone from your relative female.

Nisba: geneology.

Omda: a tribe head comes after Nazir.

Raba (rabai'a): four years old cow.

Rakuba: sun shelter.

Rushash: early rainy season.

Sabny: dry time within the rainy season.

Sarraq: thief.

Seyf hannan: very hot summer.

Seyf: summer.

Shaq: creek or valley.

Shawwir abba: take advice of my father (Ian Cunnison 1966).

Shawwir ayya: take advice of my mother.

Shedera: tree.

Shederat el juma'a: men tree.

Sot: whip.

Suwah: not rainy day.

Ta'im: delicious.

Talha: land with acacia seyal trees.

Teni (tenia): three years old cow.

Teyr el bagar: horsefly

Um hataba: a place with inpentrable, dense trees

Wali: guardian.

Wota (Mouwota): dry season journey

Wulyan: relatives

SOME TERMINOLOGIES OF MOVEMENTS:

Rahoul: is the Baggara movement from one place to another; it usually implies moving for a short distance.

Masar: is the Baggara movement from one place to another for a longer distance than *rahoul.*

Morhal: is the route Baggara follow one moving from one place to another; mostly each tribe has two *morahil* ; one for south to north movement and another one for north to south movement.

Munzala: is the new place where Baggara recently settled (*Manazil* is the plural).

Nouzoul: the act of settling in the new place.

Ratiya: coagulated sour milk.

Nasia: sour, skimmed milk mixed in water.

Gufas (sing. gafas): cages for carrying chickens from one place to another.

Da'iyyna: a moving camp.

Dara: men gathering place.

Fariq: the camp.

Fatour: breakfast.

Ghada: lunch.

Asha'a: dinner.

Safayiin: oxen saddles.

Rabita: a roll of mats (pl. *rabayit*).

Abareeg: prayer water bottles.

TYPES OF BAGGARA ROPES:

Zimil: for handling large loads.

Salab: similar to zimil.

Zomam: it is a reign for ox, passed through the nose of a tame ox.

Rasan: it is a reign for camels.

Gournat: for milking cows, one tied on the cow rear legs and one for tying the calf to the front leg.

Ouglat: (sing. Ougal) for tying the camel leg when laid on the ground.

Gayed: (pl. goyoud) hobbles for shackling camel front legs or donkey.

Um shababa: to be tied the head of unruly cow to catch her for milking.

Ripig: it is rope for tying many calves together in a single rope.

Habil el Eigal: it is rope for tying a calf to a wood or a tree.

Shabaka: is a network, placed around the mouth of, a young calf to
    prevent him from suckling.

Wajaj: it is rope made either of leather or from dom palm

Nisaah: is rope made from either leaves of dom palm or leather by
  braiding as in hair braiding.

Tujaj: it is a coiled rope used to make rope-beds.

MATS TYPES HAVE DIFFERENT NAMES:

Ab Joggie (ab joggey): mat used to cover sides of the dome.

Kattal: mat used as insulator inside the dome.

Kattal ab khashoum: front mat.

Shouga: large mat.

Haggal (Hajala): similar to Kattal.

Berish el drangal: for covering darangal (Baggara bedstead).

Berish el salah: prayer's mat.

Mufrasha: sleeping mat.

TYPES OF BEDS (ANAGREEB):

Angareb kabir – large bed, for sleeping, it is a general purpose *angareb*

Gaad – for sitting, also called (*ab'jeabey*), also used for kids as sleeping bed for young born.

Banbar – small bed exclusively used by women when cooking or
  chatting.

Angareb el khoumam - this is *angareb* used by young ladies, and brides to
    show off their luggage during migration or when the brides move
    to her husband's dome.

TYPES OF WATER SUPPLY SOURCES:

Bir: well.

Rahad: small water pool..

Bahr: river.

Birka: large water pool.

Buta: large water pool but smaller than Birka.

Dahal, plural Duhul: water pools.

Fula: water pool where water remains stagnant for long time.

Feyd: water pool in cracking clay soil areas.

Haffir: man-made water pool.

Idd: wells.

Khor: seasonal water course pr stream, valley or creek.

Mayaa: shallow lagoon.

Qelti, plural Qulati: large and deep water hole full of water.

Ragaba: stream filled from a river and running inland.

Rahad: water pool.

Rigl: small stream also means leg.

Saraf: continuously trekling stream)

Shaqq: valley.

Tumud: water hole.

Wadi: waterbed, wider than a Khor.

Biraima M. Adam

10 REFERENCES

Abdulmlik El Tahir El Mahal, 2007, *Sudanese Popular Culture: Diverse Topics.* 1s edition. Sudanese Ministry of Culture, Youth and Sports. Series 8: Culture for All, (in Arabic).

Biraima M. Adam, 2013, *Baggara of Sudan: Marriage Customs and Traditions.* Publisher Amazon.com.

Adil A. Mahmoud, 2006, *Baggara Tribes of Western Sudan: Topics in their Origin, Genealogy and Culture.* 1st edition, International Press Co., (in Arabic).

Ahmed Abdul Gadir Arbab, 1998, *Darfur History through the ages.* Unknow Publisher, (in Arabic).

Ahmed Abdulla Adam, 1997, *Sudan Tribes: Topics in Coexistence and Cohabitation,* publisher: Sudanese currency Co. Ltd., (in Arabic).

Ali H. Salelh, (2004), *The Hawazma Tribe: The Emboiement of Sudanese Identity,* publisher;. Sudanese currency Co. Ltd. (in Arabic)

Amin Hamid Zainelabidin, 2009, Abyei Crisis between International Law, and Arbitration. Publ. International Graphics, Beltsville MD 20705, USA.

Atem Mabior, 2007, Abyei Issue from a neutral perspective. Sudan Tribune. 25 November 2007.

Awad Abbaker Ismail, 2011, Silent People Speaks out: Dajo People were the First who Ruled Abyei, Sudan National Archives online resources. (In Arabic: al samitoun yatahdasoun: el Dajo hum hukam Abyei al awa'il), (in Arabic).

Barbara J. Michael, 1996, "Baggara." Encyclopedia of World Cultures. *Encyclopedia.com.* (October 20, 2012).

http://www.encyclopedia.com/doc/1G2-3458001464.html
Charlotte Hulley (2012) Youth Peacebuilding Training, Sudan. Internet resources.

Dirar Saleh Dirar, 2001, Arabic Tribes Migration to the Nile, Egypt and Sudan. Touba Library, Riyad, Suadi Arabia.

Mubarak Mahmoud Farah, 2011, Missiriyya's Blood Money Compensation, Payments and Separation of Feuding Groups (in Arabic). Unknown publisher.

Francis Mading Deng, (2009), Frontiers of Unity: An Experiment inAfro-Arab Cooperation, Routledge publ. ISBN-10: 0710313527.

Hassan Najila, 2002, *My Memories in El Badia (Subpurb).* 5th edition, Medical Science Academy Press. (in Arabic).

Ian Cunnison, (1966), Baggara Arabs: Power and the Lineage in a Sudanese Nomad Tribe, Oxford University Press.

Ismail Abeid Abbaker, 2005, Dajo: from where to where? Khartoum University Press. (in Arabic).

Janathan Owens, 1993, A grammer of Nigerian Arabic. Wieshaden – Harrassoitz.

Julie Flint and Alex De Waal, (2008), Darfur: a New History of A Long War. African Arguments, Zed Books.

Harold A. MacMichael, 1922, *A History of the Arabs in the Sudan* Vols 1, 2. Cambridge.

Harold A. MacMichael, 1967, *The Tribes of Northern and Central Kordofan*, Psychology Press, Oct 1, 1967 - 260 pages.

Kenneth David Druitt Henderson.,1956, *Sudan Republic*. London, E. Benn. Cambridge University Press. (cited by Ian Cunnison (1966).

Mohamed ibn Omar El Tunisi, 1803, Sharpening of Minds with History of Arabs Land and Sudan (in Arabic).

Mohamed Suliman, 1999, *The Nuba Mountains of Sudan: Resource access, violent conflict, and identity*, From: Cultivating Peace Conflict and Collaboration in Natural Resource Management *edited by Daniel Buckles* IDRC/World Bank 1999, ISBN 0-88936-899-6.

Mohammed Wad Dafalla Al Jaali Al Fadli, 2012, *Tabagat Book*. 3rd edition, Dar el Sudania for Book. (in Arabic).

Mohyieldin Khalil Elrayah, 2003, *Baggara Stories and Axioms*. Prepared and edited by Dr. Mohamed Abuzayd Osman. (In Arabic.

Robert O Collins., 1971, 'Land beyond the Rivers, the Southern Sudan, 1898 – 1918.' Yale University Press, New Haven and London.

Wikipedia – *Hijama*, url: http://en.wikipedia.org/wiki/Hijamah
Zanab A. Mohamed Salah, 2008, *Dress and Costumes of Baggara Tribes in Sudan: Missiriyya Tribe*. 1st edition, self-published by the Author. (in Arabic).

ABOUT THE AUTHOR

Biraima (Bir) Adam, was born to a   nomadic Baggara family, in Sudan, around 1963/1964 time frame, in one of the most remote and mountainous area, in western Centeral Sudan.   He was raising and rearing cattle with his fellow Baggara kins.

1989,   the author graduated in Khartoum Univerity, Faculty of Agriculture, Department of Foresty with the best student prize.

1993 the author completed his master degree in the Medditerranean Agronomic Institute of Chania, Greece, in the Department of Renewable Natural Resources.

In 1997, the author migrated the US where lives with his family.

2003, graduate from Unviersity of Marymount, Department of Computer Science with MS in Software Engineering.   Since then the author work as software developer, Engineer and Software Architect, to win his family bread.

To more about my life when I was a kid, one can read the Prologue of this book, which is entirely devoted to remembrance and lessons of my childhood as a young Baggara boy at that time.